The Twenty Greatest
Philosophy Books

Also available from Continuum:

Great Thinkers A–Z, edited by Julian Baginni and Jeremy Stangroom

What Philosophy Is, edited by Havi Carel and David Gamez

What Philosophers Think, edited by Julian Baggini and Jeremy Stangroom

A Brief History of Philosophy, by Derek Johnston

The Twenty Greatest Philosophy Books

James Garvey

continuum

Continuum International Publishing Group
The Tower Building   80 Maiden Lane
11 York Road   Suite 704
London SE1 7NX   New York 10038

British Library Cataloguing-in-Publication Data
A catalogue record for this book is available from the British Library.

ISBN: HB: 0-8264-9053-0
      PB: 0-8264-9054-9

Library of Congress Cataloging-in-Publication Data

Typeset by Servis Filmsetting Ltd, Manchester
Printed and bound in Great Britain by Cromwell Press Ltd, Trowbridge, Wiltshire

Contents

Introduction

It isn't easy to say what a great philosophy book is. The trouble is, at bottom, that no one really agrees about what philosophy itself is. Of course, there are clear conceptions of it, statements of what it might be or should be – philosophers, particularly the great ones, do have something to say about their discipline. There is, however, not much in the way of consensus in all of this. It is possible to discern two sorts of answer, two conceptions of philosophy. We'll think about these two answers a little, and then say something about what a great philosophy book is.

For most, philosophy is characterized by its subject matter. Philosophers deal primarily with three questions: What exists? How do we know? What are we going to do about it? The first question involves us in metaphysics, the study of existence in its most abstract sense. You can find your way into it by noticing that it is further upstream than the sciences, which begin with the existence of some bit of the world and move on from there. Metaphysics not only deals with the bare bones of reality, but it also tries to put some flesh on the bones, and in so doing it says something about what it is to be human; whether or not we are free or determined; what the relation is between mind and body; whether there is a God; what he or she might be like; what the properties of objects are; what causes and effects are; what numbers might be; and so on.

The second question – how do we know – is shorthand for epistemology, the study of knowledge and the justification of belief. Epistemology is in the business of formulating theories of knowledge, saying what the conditions are for knowing something or other, determining what truth itself is. The ancient answer to the question of knowledge, owed to Plato, is the view that knowledge consists in justified, true belief. The trouble is saying just what truth and justification are. Again, the enquiry is further upstream than other disciplines. The questions here are not, for example, on a par with the question of how we know some rock or other is 3 million years old. The task of epistemology is the more abstract one of specifying the conditions for knowing as such.

The third question – What are we going to do about it? – is probably the oldest of philosophical questions, or at least the one closest to the heart of philosophy's hero, Socrates. A large part of philosophy is an enquiry into morality, not only saying what right and wrong are, but also specifying some procedure which might help in making the right choices in life. The moral dimension of our lives can be thought of more broadly than this, of course, and philosophers have concerned themselves not just with the morally good life, but also with the best way to live. Other questions in the neighbourhood concern value itself, as well as the nature of beauty.

By now you have probably noticed that the subject matter of philosophy is abstract, but its abstraction does not consign it to irrelevancy. Philosophical questions are almost always lurking about two steps behind any other sort of question. You can suspect that a particular politician is lying. You read the newspapers and learn that some people are saying that she knew about something and tried to cover it up. Others might weigh in, and claim that she never deliberately misled anyone. You can start wondering about what a lie actually is. Whatever a lie is, you probably have to think of it as at least voluntary, as something done deliberately. What is a deliberate action? What does it mean to have an intention? If you want answers to these questions, it's no good asking a politician or a lawyer. You will need to consult philosophy. The answer you eventually plump for, it seems clear, fixes the answer you give to the original, practical question about the politician. Whether or not you think throwing her out of office is a good idea depends, ultimately, on the philosophical position you adopt.

The relevance of philosophy can be thought of in at least one other way. Philosophical questions are human questions, in the sense that being human almost requires us to wonder about them at some time or other. Kant is right when he points out that reason just cannot help itself when it comes to metaphysics. This is certainly not to suggest that each one of us settles into philosophical worries on a daily basis, but there is something to the claim that philosophy is the most human of disciplines. More or less every culture has, in its own way, wondered about the three questions scouted above. The answers given say something about those cultures, of course, but the fact that the answers were thought to be necessary in the first place says something about us humans, and also something about the relevance of philosophy generally.

The second conception of philosophy has it that philosophy has nothing to do with particular questions. One might philosophize about anything, it is sometimes said, and what matters are the methods brought to bear. Philosophy, on this view, is a certain sort of thinking, namely thinking informed by logic or at least careful reasoning. Philosophy at its best gets conclusions into clear view and supports those conclusions with arguments. Anyone can tell you that murder is wrong, but the view becomes philosophical when the claim is backed up by reasons which hang together in a certain way. Philosophers argue, and it is the practice of careful argumentation that makes philosophy what it is.

What this second view gets right is the fact that philosophy's subject matter really has changed over the millennia. The big three questions have always been with us, but philosophers have understood them in different ways, and they have also had an interest in much more. Philosophical successes, if that is what they are, sometimes involve new disciplines wandering off on their own and setting up shop outside philosophy. To name just a few, maths, psychology and, to some extent, what we call natural science were born as kinds of philosophical enquiry. In each case, what got the thing going was a certain sort of mental rigour, and perhaps philosophy is best characterized by this alone.

You can see that the two views can sometimes be at odds. If you think philosophy requires a certain concern for some particular subject matter, you might not think much of an alleged philosopher going on about the finer points of logic or the minutiae of revealed Christianity. If you think philosophy requires the use of a certain methodology, you might not think much of Hegel, Nietzsche or even Plato.

In the face of the two views, the thing to do might be just to cast the net broadly and count as philosophical anything which takes up the traditional subject matter of philosophy and at least shows a concern or preference for a certain sort of logical rigour. So far, so good. But then what counts as a great philosophy book?

Philosophical greatness, like philosophy itself, is easy to spot but not easily characterized. Influence certainly matters, and without doubt all of the books considered here have had (and still have) a large influence, both inside and outside of philosophy lecture halls. It is possible to read this book as a history of the largest philosophical ideas, captured in philosophy's most influential books. The concerns of the Ancient Greek philosophers get a fair hearing, and a consideration of Aquinas might help you to see how the ideas of the Ancients were passed on to modern thinkers. You will see the rise of reason in the modern period, in both the political philosophy of Hobbes and Rousseau and the metaphysics and epistemology of Descartes. The thinking underpinning empiricism is traced from its beginnings in Locke through to its disturbing outcome in Hume's sceptical conclusions. Kant's revolution in both epistemology and metaphysics is explored, along with its influence among philosophers in Europe and elsewhere. There is also a particular emphasis on the philosophy of the past hundred years or so. Whether or not these recent books will be judged by future philosophers as great is something we cannot yet tell, but considering them will give a sense of what philosophy is today and maybe where it is headed.

The readability of a great book should count for something too, and it does in this collection. It does not count for everything, however, because readability can be trumped by something else: intellectual power. Many, though by no means most, of the great philosophers are difficult reads, and it is possible to think that intellectual power sometimes gets in the way of literary skill. Would you have it any other way? Would you sacrifice a few of Aristotle's conclusions for an equal number of pleasing images or imaginative passages?

The difficulty of philosophy usually comes with the territory. Wittgenstein said that reading philosophy is a kind of agony. You can find a little consolation in this: if a genius like Wittgenstein found philosophy difficult, the rest of us might be excused for struggling a little too. The difficulty has something to do with the fact that philosophy has the hardest questions in it, and the further fact that thinking about them carefully is never straightforward.

Even if characterizing great philosophy precisely is beyond us, it is still true that you know it when you see it. It might be best to think of 'great philosophy' as a family resemblance term, a notion of Wittgenstein's, which we might glance at now. Wittgenstein argues that some terms pick things out because of a set of shifting properties as opposed to some single property. His example is the word 'game'. Lots of things count as games, but the games themselves share no single property in common, in virtue of which all are games. Instead they share a kind of family resemblance, as do the smiling faces in your family album. The noses might not all be the same shape, the eye colours might vary, but it's still clear that everyone in the album is related. The album of great philosophy books might be a little like this too. There are lots of different properties, but all share a kind of resemblance, a greatness you can just know when you see it.

Maybe that is a cop-out, and you are entitled to think that it is if you like. Reasonable people can argue about what counts as a great book, but no matter where you come down on the question, it seems likely that our lists of great books will have a lot in common.

We have thought a little about what philosophy is and what greatness is, and for the sake of completeness it is worth thinking for a moment about what a book is – in particular, what this book is. You know as well as I do that books which attempt to characterize large thoughts, particularly a large number of large thoughts, leave something out. This is unavoidable, and so certain judgements come into play, based on the considerations above, but also on the demands of putting everything into a coherent and, in this case, introductory book. The whole thing should gel and give the reader coming to philosophy for the first time a feel for the subject matter. It might be that Leibniz, Spinoza, Voltaire, Russell and even lesser thinkers are better philosophers than some of those included here. But if you are aiming for a decent introductory mix, you might think that leaving them out and putting others in is a good idea. No book about philosophy books can say everything worth saying about them. But this book does try to deal with the largest thoughts in those books, and it does so plainly and critically. There is no formal logic here, nor is there needless jargon. You will hear about not just the great thoughts and the arguments for them, but also the troubles associated with thinking about them. This book has objections and counter-arguments in it. It is not just a cheer for great books. It is also organized chronologically, by the publication date (as far as we know it) of the books themselves. The chapters build on each other, but each one is more or less self-contained. You can dip in where you like or read it straight through.

Some people who have dipped in and read parts of this book, and others who are owed thanks for different sorts of help, include: Laura-May Abron, Sophie Davies, Mark Hammond for insights into Nietzsche, Kim Hastilow, Ted Honderich, Julia LeMense Huff, Justin Lynas, Yolonne MacKenzie, Anthony O'Hear, Raj Sehgal for his alarmingly comprehensive grasp of Marx, Barry Smith, Jeremy Stangroom, Joanna Taylor, Slav Todorov, Jon Webber for his godlike understanding of Sartre, and Sarah Douglas at Continuum for explaining why 'deadline' has the word 'dead' in it. Those who know the secondary literature will recognize my many other debts. All mistakes in this book are theirs.

Finally, this book is dedicated to Judy Garvey, the most influential philosopher I have ever met.

1 Republic

Plato (427–347 BC)

Reasonable people can lose their composure when reflecting on Plato and his various accolades. He is generally considered to be the father of the West's intellectual heritage, a thinker who single-handedly set philosophy on a course it still follows more than two thousand years later. A. N. Whitehead memorably claimed that the safest general characterization of Western philosophy is that 'it consists of a series of footnotes to Plato'. It has been said since that this is an exaggeration, but not much of one. From our historical vantage point, Plato seems also to have the singular distinction of creating and bringing to perfection a kind of literary art, the philosophical dialogue. Even if his philosophy were of no real interest to us, his writing would still be captivating. Cicero tells us that if God were to speak, it would be in a language like Plato's. Put worries about your composure to one side. Be flabbergasted by Plato. His genius really is remarkable, his dialogues really are breathtaking, his influence really is incalculable, and philosophy really is what it is because of him. His masterpiece is the *Republic*.

By some miracle of history, we have not just the *Republic* but all the dialogues Plato wrote. The dialogues take the form of philosophical cross-examinations. A question is asked – say, What is courage? – and an answer is given. The answer is subjected to scrutiny, a series of further questions and replies are made, and eventually the original answer is found wanting in some respect. Perhaps it leads to an absurdity or contradicts something else said. A new attempt at an answer is made, in light of the recent discussion, and the process continues.

Plato's mentor, Socrates, is the hero and interrogator in most of the dialogues. We know very little about him, but we do know that he was a master of argumentation. According to Xenophon, he 'could do what he liked with any disputant'. This he did, loudly and publicly, more often than not demonstrating that the great and the good of ancient Athens really did not know what they were talking about, particularly when they talked about virtue. His enemies, who probably only wanted to shut him up, charged him with impiety and corrupting the youth of the city. Rather than abandon philosophy, he chose death, giving philosophy its first martyr and the dialogues a unique kind of poignancy. As we read about Socrates happily pursuing his definitions between the occasional cup of wine, we know it will end with a cup of poison in a prison cell.

Although there is no general agreement as to the precise chronology of the dialogues, scholars divide them into three rough groups: the early, middle and late dialogues. The early dialogues are thought to reflect the interests and views of the historical Socrates, while the Socrates of the middle and late dialogues is more and more a mouthpiece for Plato's own philosophy.

The early dialogues are inconclusive. Socrates and his fellow investigators never settle on a definition. Some see in the middle and later dialogues Plato's efforts to save his mentor from what might be regarded as a kind of failure to solve the problems posed in the early dialogues. Certainly the *Republic* can be read in this way. It is clearly a middle dialogue, with Plato now confident and at the height of his powers, moving beyond Socrates' interest in ethics and into metaphysics and epistemology, answering some of the questions his mentor first posed.

It is worth noting at the outset that the *Republic* is divided into ten books, no doubt by a later editor. The first book asks the questions the rest attempt to answer: What is justice and is being just worth the trouble? Books two through four are generally concerned with the nature of the just state, but book four begins to concentrate on justice in the individual. Books eight and nine compare justice in the city and the person. The middle books give an account of Plato's notions of political reform and, perhaps most importantly, offer a statement of his metaphysics and epistemology. The final book, which seems like a hastily compiled appendix, treats Plato's notions of art and the immortality of the soul. We will consider some of these themes in what follows.

Justice

The question of justice arises in book one with an offhand remark on the part of the ageing and wealthy merchant Cephalus, who maintains that one of the advantages of being well-heeled is that you need not lie or cheat. It is a comfort, he says, to know that you have the means to treat other people justly, to tell the truth and return what you have borrowed. The remark is enough to get Socrates going.

Suppose you borrow a weapon from a friend, Socrates says, who meanwhile goes mad. Flushed with anger and not entirely himself, maybe with homicide on his mind, he demands the return of his property. As Cephalus would have it, it is just or right to give the weapon back, but that cannot be all there is to it. A few more conventional definitions of justice are offered by others and found wanting, until the amiable mood of the conversation is broken by an outburst from the rhetorician and sophist Thrasymachus. When he wades in, it is as dramatic a moment in a philosophical conversation as one can imagine.

Thrasymachus, having had enough of the preceding high-minded talk, insists that what we call 'justice' is nothing more than self-interest. Those in power make laws which suit their own interests and aims, and justice is nothing more lofty than the codification of the will of the strong. Might really does make right. Furthermore, Thrasymachus argues that no matter what people might say in polite company, the corrupt are happiest and we generally admire them because they get what they want. Being just in the conventional sense is simply not worth it, not advantageous, not desirable. We would all rather be the money-laundering wise guy cruising the Mediterranean on his new yacht, not the just but penniless moralist. Why bother with justice and virtue when looking after your own interests leads so clearly and obviously to happiness?

Thrasymachus's outburst has echoes throughout the history of philosophy and beyond. It is the first expression of a suspicion about the foundation of morality which has grown into nihilism, ethical egoism, cynical realism, realpolitik, relativism, and much else. It takes Plato the rest of the dialogue to deal with it.

The answer begins with an unusual move on the part of Socrates. He argues that since their quarry, the nature of justice, is hard to spot, the best place to look for it is on a large scale: in the just city. Since cities and individuals can be just, what is true of one should hold true, by analogy, for the other. What, then, is the nature of the just city on Plato's view? The answer, or part of it, is more than a little alarming.

The just city

Socrates imagines the beginnings of any human collective. Human beings are not self-sufficient; we need each other and a measure of cooperation to survive. We are also naturally suited to different tasks, and efficiency counsels that individuals do what they are best suited to do. These two simple lines of thinking lead Socrates to a certain conception of justice in the ideal city. It would be unjust, maybe even a kind of theft, if a person occupied someone else's natural role. It would amount to taking something from someone else. It is best for me and for everyone else if I do what I am naturally best-suited to do. It is a short step from these thoughts to the view that justice in the city consists in everyone doing what they are naturally supposed to do.

For Plato, then, there are three classes of citizens: the guardians who rule, the auxiliaries who police and defend, and the artisans who produce goods and render services. Given Plato's conception of justice in the city, the right people must be assigned the right roles, and this is accomplished by a kind of selective breeding programme, coupled with a regime of education and indoctrination – some might say censorship, propaganda and brain-washing. Furthermore, the people need to stay in the roles to which they are assigned. Although Plato countenances the possibility of some class mobility, just any craftsman putting on airs, thinking he might make a fine ruler, simply won't do. Plato suggests that the rulers should tell a 'noble lie':

the Gods settle the fate of every individual at birth, mixing a metal into their bodies which corresponds to their class. Thus, guardians are children of gold and born to rule; auxiliaries are children of silver and born to fight; and craftsmen are children of iron or bronze and born to produce. There can be no shifting of roles, as one's place is literally constitutionally fixed or preordained.

You might be wondering, rightly, how a just city can be built on lies, censorship, propaganda and selective breeding, with the citizens programmed from birth to do just what the guardians tell them to do. Perhaps the city is just in Plato's sense, and maybe the trains run on time, but shouldn't ideal cities be more than simply stable and efficient? Shouldn't the people be happy, maybe have a little freedom, a say in how the city works? Hasn't Socrates, who objected so vigorously to Thrasymachus's outburst, fallen into advocating just what he denied earlier, that justice is nothing more than obeying the will of the powerful?

There is a kind of response to this, and it might not exactly work, but we will have a look at it anyway. Plato argues that the ideal city cannot be a reality until philosophers become kings, until the ones in charge have a share in wisdom, particularly an understanding of what goodness really is. The rulers are not mere tyrants, but individuals who by nature and nurture are best placed to choose what is in the interests of everyone. Lies and eugenics aside, maybe the people really will be happy, as they will be looked after by those trained to consider their interests. This is not simply obeying the will of the strong, but being governed by the ones who know best. Perhaps more details of the nature of the knowledge the rulers allegedly have will help.

The theory of forms

Plato proposes a number of analogies in books six and seven, all designed to make clear the sort of knowledge required by the rulers, the knowledge of the Good. To make sense of this, we will need to consider Plato's theory of forms, and you can find your way into it by thinking about the following problems. We call lots of different things 'red', but how did we manage to learn the meaning of the word when we are never presented with an unambiguous example of redness? Red things in the world are round and red or juicy and red or crunchy and red. How, then, did we ever learn to use the world correctly? Or think about our knowledge of something red, say the knowledge that this apple is red. It is clear that it will not be red for long; apples rot, after all, and eventually it will be brown, maybe decomposing into something we would not even call an apple any more. Consider these two questions. As the apple rots, what standard do we use to determine whether or not it is red? It seems that we need some unchanging standard, some fixed redness, but what could fit the bill in this changing world of rotting apples? Second, if we really know something, it is hard to see how that knowledge could turn false. Opinions might turn out false, but if something is known – squares have four sides or $2 + 2 = 4$, say – it has to be true forever. Again, nothing in this changing world seems able to shore up the permanency of knowledge.

Plato's remarkable solution to these problems is the theory of forms: the view that unchanging, perfect exemplars of such things as the Forms of Redness, Justice, Beauty and so on really exist in a world distinct from our own. All red things have a share in or participate in the Form of Red; all just acts, people and cities share in the Form of Justice, and so on. The forms are conceptual realities, and just as sunlight renders visible the objects of this world, knowledge of the Good enables the philosopher king to 'see' the world of forms. An enlightened ruler, then, knows what is good for everyone, and governs accordingly.

The cave metaphor is perhaps Plato most famous image, and he uses it to convey all sorts of things about the relation between this world and the world of forms, as well as the nature of the philosophical enlightenment required of the philosopher kings. He imagines prisoners chained to the floor of a cave. Immediately behind them is a raised platform, where various objects are carried back and forth, and just behind this procession is a fire. The set-up is such that the prisoners can only see the shadows of objects before them, and this they take to be reality. By some miracle, a prisoner frees himself, sees what is going on, and realizes that he has been mistaking mere illusions for real objects. He drags himself out of the cave, into the blinding light of the sun and, eventually, sees the true nature of the world.

For Plato, we are like prisoners in the cave, and this world of physical objects is merely a procession of shadows compared to the unchanging world of perfect forms. The philosopher who manages to free himself and look upon the objects outside the cave, the forms themselves, finally sees the sun, the Form of Goodness, which illuminates all. It is worth noting that the philosopher has to return to the cave – no doubt he would rather stay outside in restful contemplation – to free us. And freeing the crowd is no easy job. He suffers, being taken for a lunatic with his talk of the so-called 'real world'. Plato is here suggesting that the philosopher king rules out of a sense of duty to his subjects and has their best interests at heart. What he wants, more than the joy attending the contemplation of the forms, is justice for the city.

It is a nice image, but what truth is there in Plato's theory of forms? Perhaps the largest objection to the view, considered by Plato himself, is the Third Man Argument, which runs as follows. Beautiful things in this world are beautiful only insofar as they have a share in the Form Beautiful. The Form Beautiful itself is beautiful, Plato admits. Does this not require a third thing, a third form, which the Beautiful itself resembles? Socrates and Plato are both men insofar as they have a share in the Form Man. The Form Man must also have a share in manhood, just as the Form Beautiful is beautiful. Does this not require a third man which the Form Man must resemble for it to be a man? And isn't this third man itself a man? Reflection on the theory of forms seems to generate an embarrassing vicious regress.

You can wander into other sorts of trouble too, if you start wondering about the perfect and unchanging Form of Acne or worry a little about the forms of things which do not yet exist. Has there always been a form of Interplanetary Teleportation Device? Could Plato have contemplated it?

Justice in the individual

Put these worries to one side for the moment and recall the just city. The just city, on Plato's view, is one in which the three classes do what they are supposed to do: the classes stay in their proper place, perform their proper roles and do not interfere with one another. Having discovered justice in the city, Plato turns to justice in the individual. By analogy to the just city, a just person has three parts which must work together. Reason, spirit and appetite, for Plato, correspond to the classes of citizen in the city. A just person's inner life is structured like social life in a just city – the parts of her mind are in a similar kind of balance.

The symmetry between the parts of a person and the parts of a city is pleasing, but how much weight can the analogy bear? Many have argued that human psychology cannot really be reducible to only three principles – and it nearly goes without saying that societies are no less complex. Others note that arguments by analogy just cannot do the sort of heavy lifting required here.

Despite these worries, we now know what Plato thinks justice is, but what of his second question: Is justice worthwhile or desirable? Plato takes it that proving this amounts to showing that the just person is the happiest sort of person and that the just state has the happiest people in it. He attempts to do this by considering all sorts of unjust people and unjust political organizations. In each case, his aim is to show that compared to a just person or city, the unjust version has less happiness in it.

He proposes some specific arguments too. A just person escapes a kind of inner conflict, conducive to unhappiness, when the rational part of her mind rules the others. Thus, justice brings happiness, a sort of happiness unavailable to a person whose mind is tugged this way and that. Plato also argues that the parts of the person have particular, corresponding desires – the appetitive part loves gain, the spirited part loves honour, and the rational part loves wisdom. Disputes between the parts of the mind require the best judge to resolve them, and only the rational part knows the kinds of desires proper to each part of the mind. Therefore, reason is the best judge when it comes to the satisfaction of desire, and the person whose reason is in charge, the just person, will find the most satisfaction in life.

You can have some worrying thoughts about all of this. You can think that Plato has departed from ordinary morality, the everyday conception of justice. He is talking about something else when he discusses reason ruling the other parts of the mind. You might be thinking, too, that the totalitarian utopia he envisions cannot be a just state. You can go on thinking this if you like, but it will take more than thoughts to answer Plato. He has levelled arguments for his views, and what is needed to reply to him are arguments, not merely discomfited thoughts. You might lose your composure again if you think that almost everyone since Plato has had just the same worrying thoughts, and other thoughts besides, on reading his dialogues. Perhaps much of philosophy since has been engaged in turning such thoughts into proper replies to Plato.

2 Nicomachean Ethics
Aristotle (384–322 BC)

Aristotle, like Plato, is an intellectual anomaly. His genius seems inexplicable. Plato, we have noted, invented and perfected a form of art, the philosophical dialogue. Aristotle invented not only whole disciplines, but the very idea of a discipline itself. He was the first to identify the history, proper assumptions and aims of a host of intellectual pursuits, bringing into being the organized study of biology, politics, metaphysics, physics, maths, psychology, poetry, rhetoric, ethics, aesthetics, logic, meteorology, geology, methodology, cosmology and theology. It is difficult to believe that a single human mind could have done so much.

Moreover, ancient commentators put him in the same literary league as Plato, characterizing his writing as 'a golden river of eloquence.' They distinguished between his esoteric and exoteric writings. The former are technical works in progress written for use by students and colleagues within his school, the Lyceum. The latter are well-crafted, beautifully written pieces, designed for public consumption. Many hearts have fallen on the discovery that the golden river of eloquence is lost to us; not a fragment of his public writings survives.

We are left with the works in progress – what might well have been his lecture notes – and only the most fervent Aristotelian apologist could insist that these works are beautiful in the literary sense. The writing is full of technical vocabulary, tight argumentation, and terse references to other thinkers or schools of thought – all of which would have been welcomed by his intended audience but might leave today's readers baffled. The arguments come thick and fast and style is certainly sacrificed for clarity, rigour and precision. It is possible to pine for the golden river, particularly late at night when stuck on some difficult argument in the Aristotelian corpus. When the sun comes up and the cobwebs clear, though, there is reason enough to be thankful for what we have. Although the going is tough, Aristotle's surviving works are among the greatest pieces of philosophy ever written.

Perhaps the most interesting, readable and influential part of the surviving corpus is *Nicomachean Ethics*, named after Aristotle's son Nicomachus who edited the work. It is of a piece with Aristotle's other writings, in the sense that it is teleological in flavour. Aristotle's thinking is saturated by the notions of aims, goals and ends. In his physics, for example, we find the view that objects move as they do because they have a natural place in the physical world. The natural place of fire is in the heavens, so flames aim towards the heavens or rise; the natural place of a stone is the earth, so stones head downwards or fall. In a certain sense, objects move as they do because of their natural inclinations or aims.

Causes, purposes and ends

A consideration of Aristotle's four causes, or four explanatory features of a thing, might clarify this a little. To understand some object or other, we might ask four sorts of questions. To borrow Aristotle's example, we can ask four questions about a statue. What is it made of (bronze: its material cause); what sort of thing is it (a statue: its formal cause); what brought it into being or initiated the changes that led to its being what it is (a sculptor: its efficient cause); and what is it for (decoration: its final cause)? Whereas modern thinkers might be content with understanding just the physical facts of a thing – facts about an object's composition, say – Aristotle goes further with the last two sorts of cause, the efficient and final causes. In thinking about these, we come to know what a thing is for, what it aims at, what its purpose is, and also what is instrumental in its achieving that purpose. These sorts of facts are not what modern minds would consider as on a par with the physical facts of composition. Indeed, modern minds since Darwin have been doing all they can to stop viewing the world and the things in it as full of purpose or aiming at something. For Aristotle, however, facts about purposes are just as important as what we call physical facts, perhaps more so. They are in the world for us to discover, too, just as physical facts are.

Not just statues and stones, but plants, animals and human beings are goal-directed things as well. Aristotle does not mean by this that plants have individual aims or intentions; they do not form the conscious thought that climbing up the wall would be a fun thing to do. Rather, an acorn, for example, contains within it the goal or end of becoming an oak tree, but not the intention of becoming an oak tree. In just this sense, human beings are for something, have an aim or purpose, and it is with such purpose in the general sense that *Nicomachean Ethics* is concerned.

You can hear something of this in the very first lines of the book. Here, Aristotle claims that in every art, investigation, action or pursuit, we aim at some good. There is a sense in which our aims would be circular and ultimately pointless if they were just directed at each other, at other minor ends. If I just did this for that, and that for something else, and that something else for another something, which might turn out just to be the original goal, with no supreme or general goal in mind, then I am going around in little circles. All of the little goals I have must themselves aim at some supreme goal, what Aristotle calls the Good; otherwise I am left with a potential infinity of minor aims and no chance of an ultimate purpose to my actions. I might pursue some actions for money, others for health, others for social standing, but unless all these sub-goals aim at something desirable for its own sake, I am actually pursuing nothing. Aristotle argues that an infinite progression of aims with no stopping point is itself pointless.

Happiness

The ultimate aim is what Aristotle calls 'the good for man'. This, he notes, is what everyone calls 'happiness'. Aristotle then defines happiness as 'an activity of the soul in accordance with perfect virtue', and unpacking this definition takes him the bulk of the book. It is worth noting immediately that one can get into difficulties of interpretation if Aristotle is taken to mean by 'soul' and 'virtue' what we mean by them. Translators fall over themselves in the many introductions to the book to warn the reader that the Greek words *psychē* and *aretē*, usually rendered as 'soul' and 'virtue' respectively, are not easily translated into English.

Aristotle's conception of soul is not lumbered with two thousand years of Christian theology as is ours. For him, having a soul does not mean being inhabited by some ghostly, immortal spirit which somehow operates or animates the body. It is just being alive, being able to undertake certain characteristic activities. The plant soul is vegetative, that is to say that living plants are capable of growth, able to take on nutrients. The animal soul is, among other things, sensitive; distinctive of animals is their capacity to perceive the world by means of their senses. The human soul is distinctive in that it is rational or at least partly rational, and therefore the distinctive human activity has something to do with reasoning or thinking.

Aristotle's conception of virtue has more to do with excellence than saintliness – with exercising some distinctive capacity well, rather than being a goody-two-shoes. Aristotle is therefore perfectly happy to talk about a virtuous knife, a knife that is quite sharp and therefore excellent for the activities distinctive of knives. A virtuous horse is possible for Aristotle too – it is a horse that performs those activities characteristic of horses very well. Perhaps it can clear higher jumps than other horses. A virtuous human, then, is someone who performs distinctly human activities very well. A virtuous human is an excellent thinker.

Aristotle's conception of happiness – an activity of the soul in accordance with perfect virtue – is therefore much broader than the translations suggest. He is not talking simply of moral virtues, but human excellence generally conceived. His aim is nothing less than to offer an account of what it is to live a human life well, and for Aristotle this is something more than simply living a morally good life.

This is of course not to say that morality has no place in a happy human life. There are two sorts of virtues in the Aristotelian sense – moral virtues and intellectual virtues – and a flourishing life requires both. Given that rationality is what makes human beings distinctive, being a happy human consists in reasoning well. This manifests itself in both action and thought. A happy human, then, is one who acts in accordance with reason and a consideration of such action amounts to an account of morality or moral virtue. A happy human is also one who engages in fine thinking, one who makes good use of her mind. A consideration of this sort of activity amounts to an account of intellectual virtue. We will consider Aristotle's account of moral virtue first.

The Doctrine of the Mean

There is, however, a worry associated with Aristotle's talk of moral virtue, and it is best to have it on the table right away. What readers of moral philosophy are usually after is something in the way of advice, some decision procedure or method one might use to determine the morally correct course of action. Telling us how best to live a morally good life is, after all, the point of moral philosophy, or so some maintain. But does Aristotle give us any moral advice at all? And if he does not, is the *Nicomachean Ethics* a kind of failure?

He seems to defend the Doctrine of the Mean, the claim that the morally right thing to do is the middle course between extremes. The meat of the doctrine consists in Aristotle's claim that 'virtue . . . is a state of character concerned with choice, lying in a mean . . .. [I]t is a mean between two vices, that which depends on excess and that which depends on defect'. Those who seek moral advice typically interpret Aristotle as saying that if you want to do what is right, choose the mean. Some examples will make this clear.

How should the virtuous person face death? There are two extremes in the attitudes one might take towards death: on the extreme of excess is the vice of rashness and on the extreme of defect is the vice of cowardice, but in the middle is the virtue of courage. Boldly but stupidly dashing into the enemy ranks is as much a vice as cowering behind a shrub. The right thing to do is something in the middle of these extremes. How should the virtuous person talk about herself? Again there are two extremes: vanity and inappropriate humility, and in the middle is a kind of honesty about oneself and one's achievements, which Aristotle calls 'proper pride'.

We need to make two provisos before getting on to the question of the worth of the Doctrine of the Mean as a piece of moral advice. First of all, Aristotle is not talking about an arithmetical mean. He is not suggesting that when presented with ten bottles of wine one ought to choose the mean and drink five. Rather, the mean varies from person to person, changes given the vagaries of circumstance; it is, as Aristotle says, the mean relative to us. To feel and act 'when one should, and in the conditions and towards the people and for the end and in the way one should – that is the middle and best course'. Second, for some actions Aristotle notes that there just is no mean. There is no middle ground when it comes to murder or rape, for example.

Is the doctrine a piece of moral advice? Many think it is, and the 'Golden Mean', as it is sometimes called, has been taken by some Christian thinkers who later appropriated Aristotle as a kind of general insistence on temperance. But is the doctrine of any real help? Suppose you are genuinely worried about making a moral mistake. Maybe you are contemplating the poor of Africa, and you wonder whether or not to forgo your holiday and give the money to charity. You seek my counsel and, after a period of reflection, I say to you, 'Observe the mean. Do what you should when you should, and in the conditions and towards the people and for the end and in the way you should, for that is the middle end best course.' You might be forgiven for thinking that I did not take you seriously at all.

The doctrine appears empty, looks like it cannot deliver if we take it to be a guide to action. So some thinkers argue that Aristotle is not giving advice but analysing the nature of virtue – describing not pre-scribing. Some locate Aristotle's moral advice elsewhere, in his view that a virtuous character is something achieved by habituation, by regularly acting virtuously. If there is any advice here at all, Aristotle might be suggesting that if you want to acquire virtue, you should imitate a virtuous person, do virtuous deeds, and eventually a virtuous character will come along for the ride. But if I really don't know what virtue is, how am I to spot the virtuous person in the first place? This might well be another dead end. The question of the value of Aristotle's consideration of moral virtue as a piece of moral advice remains an open one.

Contemplation

What of intellectual virtue? Aristotle distinguishes between two rational parts of the mind: the calculative and contemplative. The former is concerned with action – in particular, action based on sound thinking. The latter is concerned with something closer to pure contemplation or reflection on known truths. A human possessed of intellectual virtue, then, is one whose actions are guided by clear-headed thinking and who engages in theoretical reflection. It is clear that there is some overlap between moral virtue and intellectual virtue, at least as far as the calculative part of the mind goes. Choosing the mean requires a certain amount of calculative skill. But Aristotle's talk of contemplation and its role in a happy human life can jar a little. Is Aristotle saying that a person is not really happy unless he spends some time reflecting on known scientific or theoretical facts? Aristotle actually says this and more.

Recall Aristotle's interest in ends, purpose and distinctive activity. Human beings are distinctive insofar as we are rational creatures. Happiness, for Aristotle, is an activity in accord with our distinctive virtue, our rationality. The virtue associated with the best in us, the highest virtue, brings with it the best sort of happiness, perfect happiness. This, for Aristotle, is nothing less than contemplation, for the contemplative part of us is best. The highest good, the best life, the happiest life, therefore, is the contemplative life. You can take this conclusion in at least two different directions.

First, you can follow those who object on a variety of grounds. You can try counter-exampling his conclusion to death, by imagining all sorts of happy people who spend no time in contemplation, for example – maybe you can imagine happy idiots or at least happy people with no interest at all or access to scientific truths. You can object on the grounds that Aristotle has failed to identify what is distinctive about us – maybe it is not reason that is highest or best in us. You can say that happiness has more things in it than a certain sort of thinking – maybe there are other sorts of goods for us. You can bite all sorts of bullets and argue that, say, bodily pleasures are preferable to intellectual ones. All of these objections have ready replies in Aristotle's writings, and you will be unsurprised to learn that there are replies to these replies.

Or you might snuggle up to Aristotle's conception of the happiest life. Many find something ennobling and true in the view that the life of the mind is the highest sort of life; one difficulty is finding a reasonable gloss on 'highest'. You can try to temper his conclusion a little by finding a more relaxed conception of the happiest life which lets in more than just the contemplative variety. You might even think that Aristotle has got it just right and that no addenda are required at all.

It is hard to think that Aristotle himself thought he had it just right. It is difficult to imagine him satisfied with his understanding of any subject. Despite his claims about the contemplative life, it is nearly impossible to think of him resting and simply contemplating, rather than continuing with his investigations. At the very end of the *Nicomachean Ethics*, the largest and most complete account of ethics in existence at the time, he writes, 'Come, let us get on with the enquiry.' It is difficult to put the book down and do anything less.

3   Summa Theologiae
St Thomas Aquinas (1224/6–74)

Aquinas's written output is extraordinary, both in size and the range of its subject matter. Although he died before he was 50, we have over 8 million of his words – commentaries on the gospels and the writings of Aristotle, treatments of Peter Lombard's *Sentences*, disputations on truth, the soul and the nature of evil, among much else. Standing above it all are two *Summae* or *Summations*, comprehensive treatises on Catholic theology.

The first is *Summa Contra Gentiles* (*Summation of the Catholic Faith Against the Unbelievers*), which is motivated, no doubt, by Thomas's Dominican view that one should stand ready to defend one's religious beliefs through discourse with those outside of the faith. It is also true that Aquinas was motivated by reading Aristotle and the commentaries on his work written by Arabic philosophers. At the time, it was not entirely clear how best to deal with thinkers of clearly remarkable stature who nevertheless wrote and thought outside of the faith. It would not do, Aquinas thought, simply to reject them out of hand. He found truths in their writings, and thought them examples of reason getting underway without the help of scripture. Aquinas certainly distinguishes between the truths of revelation and those arrived at by natural reason, but he is unique in his time for taking the latter very seriously and, in so doing, attempting to blend the rationality of non-Christians into the theology of Christianity. He argues that revealed truths are not contrary to reason, but that reason can only prove a part of Christian doctrine. Thus he tries to show that reason can demonstrate the existence of God and the immortality of the soul to the unbeliever, but revelation is required to secure further claims – for example, that God is a Trinity or that Christ is God made flesh.

The second book is *Summa Theologiae* (*Summation of Theology*), written as a kind of encyclopedia for those already convinced of the Catholic faith. It has some of the arguments originally formulated in the earlier *Summa Contra Gentiles*, but now Aquinas is clearly writing for the converted. Although condensed versions are now available, the original runs to several volumes. If the size does not put you off, the structure of the work might. It is written as a series of 'articles', hundreds of them, each comprised of questions followed by pages of detailed summary of answers and the views of other philosophers and theologians, who are often quoted at length, along with objections to the various views and further replies. Buried in each article is Aquinas's own answer or set of answers, and teasing out his views from the rest is never a simple exercise. It might alarm you to learn that the enormous work was not the end of the matter from Aquinas's point of view. It was unfinished at his death. Following a religious experience while attending Mass, he wrote nothing more, saying only that 'All that I have written seems to me like straw compared to what has now been revealed to me.' A few months later, en route to a church council, he was struck on the head by an overhanging branch and died shortly afterwards.

The book treats a huge number of topics. Aquinas deals in part with Christian metaphysics and epistemology, taking in the existence of God, the nature of God, God's knowledge, the nature of the created order and the place of angels and human beings in it, the soul and the freedom of the human will, human nature generally, as well as some reflection on divine government. Other, possibly lesser discussions centre around ethics, expounding Aquinas's influential views on custom, habits and law, as well as virtues, along with detailed treatments of particular matters of Christian doctrine. It goes almost without saying that we can do no more here than glance at a part of all of this.

Aquinas first takes up the definition of theology and distinguishes it from philosophy. Philosophy, he argues, is human reason acting on its own to discover truth, but theology is human reason acting in the light of divine revelation. While philosophy can secure knowledge of nature, even of the existence of God, theology is in the business of understanding not just nature, but the supernatural, insofar as this is possible, through reflection backed up by scriptural authority. In particular, theology deals with the knowledge required for salvation. Most thinkers at the time just took it for granted that revealed knowledge trumps philosophical knowledge, but Aquinas is careful to think of the relation between the two sorts of knowledge and argue that they are generally compatible. Revelation does not undermine philosophy; it perfects or completes it, fills in some of the spiritual blanks which lie beyond the reach of human reason.

The Five Ways

Aquinas notes that the proposition 'God exists' is not self-evident to us, and he was, therefore, moved to attempt a demonstration of it. You can detect more than a little Aristotelian thinking in his proofs, the famous Five Ways. Aristotle claims that one must recognize the difference between what is to be assumed and what is to be proven, before theorizing can get going. Knowledge builds on itself, and some disciplines nearer the top of the edifice are dependent on the truths below; they get going with assumptions grounded elsewhere. Nearer the foundations of the structure are truths every rational person just has to accept if he or she wants to be rational. You cannot take part in a reasoned debate, for example, if you do not buy into the Law of the Excluded Middle: there is nothing between the assertion and the denial of a proposition. Only 'yes' or 'no' count as answers to questions of the form: 'Is it true that p?' If you do not accept that minimal requirement of rationality, you are doing something other than thinking reasonably. Assenting to some rules or facts is just part of the nature of rationality.

Each of the Five Ways begins with some truth or fact which everyone has to accept, and argues backwards from that truth as an effect of the power or agency of God to the existence of God. The thinking is Aristotelian, but Aquinas has other reasons for arguing backwards in this way. As we will see in a moment, for Aquinas our knowledge of God is severely circumscribed. If we can have little or no positive insight into God's nature, we cannot argue for the existence of God from God as a cause to observable effects. For both reasons, we must work backwards, from the effects of God to his existence.

Aquinas first argues from the fact that things move to the conclusion that there must be some first, unmoved mover who gets the ball rolling. Whatever is moved is moved by something else – nothing moves itself. This chain of movers and things moved cannot go on to infinity, because then nothing would actually be moving. There must be some first mover, and he concludes that this must be God.

The second argument concerns efficient causes, an Aristotelian conception of events or agents which initiate change or bring something about. Nothing can be the efficient cause of itself – nothing can bring itself about – because this would require the thing to exist before itself, and that is impossible. If there was no first efficient cause, there would be no intermediate causes, which is to say that nothing would change or be brought about. But plainly there are things which change and things have been brought about, so there must be a first efficient cause, 'which everyone gives the name of God'.

Third, Aquinas argues that everything we see is contingent, and by this he means that everything around us is merely possible: it either might be or might not be. It is stuff which comes into being and passes out of being. Contingent things only come into existence through something already existing – eggs pop out of chickens, chicks pop out of eggs, fruit grows on the vine, and so on. If everything were contingent, if everything could either be or not be, then at some point there would have been nothing. If at some point nothing existed, and if contingent things only come into existence through something already existing, then there would not be the contingent things which in fact exist all around us. So there has to be something which is not just possible, is not just contingent, but necessary. Only one thing has of itself its own necessity, and this, again, Aquinas calls 'God'.

Fourth, we find gradations in the qualities of things in the world: some things are more or less good, noble, true, and so on. Saying that something is more or less good than something else depends on there being some maximum standard, something perfectly good. Something is hotter than something else if it is closer in hotness to a further thing which is hottest. Saying or judging that something is better than something else depends on there being a standard of goodness, and so too with all other perfections. This maximally perfect something, Aquinas argues, is God.

Fifth, Aquinas, again under the influence of Aristotle, argues that things in nature act to achieve particular purposes, even though those things lack awareness. Objects tend towards ends – an oak seedling, if all goes well, grows into an oak tree. Even lifeless things seem to serve purposes. Aquinas argues that there must be some intelligence directing an otherwise blind nature towards the ends we see realized all around us. This intelligence can only be God.

Philosophers have attacked all of Aquinas's arguments, and probably the most damaging objections come in two forms. First, even if Aquinas's arguments establish something, that something need not be the existence of God as traditionally conceived. The arguments purport to prove that God exists but, even if the arguments work, they deliver something less. The first three arguments issue in the conclusion that there exists an unmoved mover, a first cause, or a necessary being. Aquinas is getting closer with talk of a maximally perfect something or an intelligence. Still, the move at the end of each argument – 'and this we all call "God"' – seems extravagant. Could there not be many uncaused causes at the back of the chain, rather than one God? Why think the uncaused cause, if there is just one, has the many attributes of the Christian God? Why think it is all-knowing, all-powerful and all-good? Maybe it is a rather pedestrian uncaused cause: without much in the way of rationality, only just powerful enough to get things rolling, possibly with malice on its mind.

Second, a number of the arguments depend on the claim that an infinite regress is unthinkable or that an infinite regress is an obvious absurdity, but it certainly does seem possible to think of the universe as always existing or its parts as always moving back through an infinite stretch of time. In this connection a certain inconsistency is also pointed out. Aquinas does seem to argue that, for example, nothing moves itself or nothing causes itself, but then concludes that there must be some unmoved or self-moving thing, some uncaused or self-causing thing. If we have to take as true the premise that nothing moves or causes itself, we seem to have to look away from its truth when contemplating the conclusion that an unmoved mover or an uncaused cause exists.

The nature of God

Aquinas, though, moves on to a consideration of God's nature, and here he identifies and elaborates on several attributes of God. He argues that God's simplicity arises from the fact that he is not corporeal and therefore has no parts. Something is good insofar as it has being or lacks nothing, and God as fully or supremely actual is therefore supremely good. God's infinity is understood in terms not of quantity but of form, and here Aquinas argues that God's form is infinite. God is also immanent, in the sense that God is present to all things as the source of their being, but given his immutable nature, God nevertheless stands outside of time and space. Finally, Aquinas argues that God is a unity; there can be only one God.

Despite the details, Aquinas argues that the essence of God can never be fully grasped by our finite intellects, unless God reveals himself to the blessed by grace. The many particular properties attributed to God both by scholars and in the Bible can be understood sometimes negatively: we can say that God is not anywhere or anytime. It would be a mistake, though, to conclude that we can say nothing positive. It might be true that we cannot fully grasp the precise sense in which God is perfectly good, Aquinas argues, but we can express positive claims about God analogically, in the recognition that the perfections attributed to God exist in him in the highest or fullest sense.

The nature of God's knowledge is also dealt with in some detail, although Aquinas argues that we can have only an analogical grip on its nature. God knows everything, Aquinas argues, but he does not express the notion in terms of propositions. Instead, God knows everything in the sense in which an architect knows everything about a building. The architect's knowledge brings the building into being – he need not build it first and then study it to know it. Similarly, God's knowledge cannot depend on the prior existence of everything, as perhaps a person living in a building might have knowledge of the structure which depends on the prior existence of the structure. God's knowledge brings about what exists.

If God knows everything, then he knows what human beings will do before they do it, and you can wonder about the sense in which human beings can be free in the face of such knowledge. You can become particularly worried about the rationality of divine punishment and reward if it turns out that God's knowledge somehow fixes human action. How can we be reasonably judged if God's knowledge settles our destinies in the first place? Aquinas claims that God's knowledge of human action is like the vision of a person at the top of a hill who looks down at those walking along a winding path to the top. From that vantage point, the individual can see all of the walkers, even though each of the walkers cannot see all the others. Similarly, we cannot see beyond the present, but God, like the person at the top of the hill, can 'see' the whole show at once – all past, present and future actions. Just because a person on the hillside sees all the acts of walking in the present, those many acts are not determined by being seen. Just because God 'sees' every action in the past, present and future, those actions need not be determined by his knowing about them. You can wonder whether or not this move works and trouble yourself, if you like, by trying to square this analogy of the hillside spectator with the analogy of the architect.

Some philosophers have little time for Aquinas. It is certainly true that his reputation was not assured until the end of the nineteenth century, when Pope Leo XIII moved theologians to take an interest in Aquinas's work. Many outside the faith, though, take *Summa Theologiae* to be something other than philosophy. Philosophy, it is argued, is a disinterested search for truth, with each premise or presupposition subject to rational scrutiny. Aquinas, however, already has the presupposed truth of the Bible in view, and the philosophy undertaken, such as it is, only serves to support truths never in doubt in the first place. You can take this point and nevertheless try to extract arguments from his writings and weigh them up without reference to the faith itself. You can also find in Aquinas a clear understanding of Aristotle, as well as treatments of human nature and government which are as philosophically rigorous as anything written inside or outside the Church.

Engaging in this sort of thing, though, does a kind of violence to Aquinas. Far better, maybe, to shift in your chair a little uncomfortably and wonder whether philosophy really is a disinterested search for truth. Aquinas certainly has a set of clearly articulated presuppositions. Is this any worse than our mistaking a weak grasp of our secular presuppositions for disinterest? Maybe that is too uncomfortable, and probably it overlooks the fact that philosophy really is willing to scrutinize more or less any premiss, no matter what it is. It is difficult to imagine Aquinas joining us in that sort of undertaking.

4   Meditations on First Philosophy
René Descartes (1596–1650)

Imagine having been schooled by fierce Jesuits who seemed not only to know absolutely everything but also to have divine authority behind them. They taught you that the earth is at the very centre of the created order. The sun, planets and sphere of the heavens revolve in perfect circles around you. When you look at a sunrise, you really see the sun moving up and away from the horizon. When you watch the constellations make their way across the night sky, they really are moving around you, the stationary centre of creation.

Now think of what it would do to you to grow up and read the reports of Galileo, to discover that the heavenly bodies are not perfect spheres – they are actually a little squashed and jagged – their orbits are not perfectly circular and the earth is probably just a planet like any other in orbit around the sun, and the sun itself is at the centre of things. Your eyes are deceiving you every time you view a sunrise, every time you see the stars apparently moving. Can you come close to imagining what it would be like to discover that everything you thought you knew about your place in the universe is just plain wrong?

If so, you have something of a grip on Descartes' motivation for writing the *Meditations*. It is probably the most important book of the modern period. Many scholars take it that modern philosophy begins with its publication. In it, the human race grows up a little, breaks with the methods and preoccupations of ancient and medieval thinkers. Descartes saw the edifice of human knowledge shaken by the new science of astronomy, and his aim in the *Meditations* was to see to it that this sort of thing never happened again.

Descartes' method

His model is mathematics. Descartes was a mathematician of extra-ordinary genius, and this might go some way towards explaining why he saw the methods of mathematics as something one might generally apply to other attempts at understanding. In the *Discourse on Method*, he lays out what he takes to be the formal steps of right reasoning, and it is possible to hear in them echoes of the steps of a mathematical proof. He lists four rules for the direction of thought:

(1) Accept nothing as true which is not presented to the mind so clearly and distinctly that there is no reason to doubt it.
(2) Break problems down into as many smaller problems as possible.
(3) Begin with what is most simple and easily understood and build on this by degrees to larger and more complex matters.
(4) Review the entire chain of thinking to ensure nothing is omitted.

Meditations is Descartes' attempt to follow these rules and, through their use, 'establish something firm and lasting in the sciences'. The book is written as a series of bedtime notes in a diary – six meditations, all of them in the first person. Descartes writes as though he is working through all of this for the first time, and there is something about this style that draws in the reader. When Descartes gets worried about whether or not he really knows something, you can find yourself worrying too. If you are in the right mood and have the right concerns, the *Meditations* is a gripping page-turner.

The book begins with a clear nod to the first rule: accept nothing as true which is not presented to the mind so clearly and distinctly that there is no reason to doubt it. Descartes is not just talking about 'reasonable doubt' here. The stakes are high, after all, and the aim is to find absolute certainty, a foundation on which to build a whole system of science. Any reason for doubt, no matter how bizarre, will do to render a belief suspect. Descartes' method, then, is the method of doubt. If a belief is to stand up to Descartes' test, it must be beyond even the shadow of a doubt. Sifting through beliefs individually would be an endless task, so Descartes sets out to find certainty by casting doubt on whole classes of beliefs.

The destruction of beliefs

Descartes begins with beliefs based on sense perception. Most of the things he thinks he knows are beliefs acquired through the use of the senses, but the senses are sometimes deceptive. Have a look at an oar halfway immersed in water and it appears bent. Think about tricks of light, mirages in the desert or the illusion of shimmering water on hot tarmac in the distance. If the senses sometimes deceive us, Descartes argues, it is a mark of prudence never to trust in them fully. Should we conclude, therefore, that none of our beliefs based on sensory evidence are certain? Should you say, based on these reflections, that you can doubt that you are holding this book in your hands?

Descartes does not think the argument can prove this much. The illusions under consideration seem to depend on less than optimal sensory conditions. When the lighting is good and an object is right in front of you, it is hard to think that tricks of the light can give you a reason to doubt what you are seeing. Anyway, we only come to realize that illusions exist by relying on our senses. I know the oar is not really bent, despite my visual experience, by touching it or maybe bringing it out of the water and subjecting it to a more careful inspection. We are aware of sensory illusion precisely because we do sometimes trust our senses. So an argument from illusion cannot cast doubt on all sensation. It depends on the veracity of sense perception in the first place.

Descartes goes so far as to say that he would have to be slightly crazy to think that these are not his hands holding the paper as he reviews his meditations by the light of the fire. You can smirk a little with him, perhaps casting a reassuring glance at your own hands holding his book; but the smirk can fade very quickly.

How many times, Descartes asks, has he dreamt that he was seated by the fire, writing or reading, innocently viewing what he thought were his hands, when in fact he was actually sound asleep and not looking at anything at all? Dreams can seem, for the dreamer at the time, as real as any waking experience. Are you certain that those are your hands holding this book, or might your hands be tucked underneath your pillow? Maybe you do not have hands at all. Telling yourself that the senses are trustworthy when conditions are good is less than reassuring once you realize that you can dream of good conditions. The situation gets a lot worse if you cannot come up with a way of distinguishing between waking and dreaming experiences. If you do not have that, if you do not have some criterion you can use to tell the difference between the two states, then for any belief you have, you simply might have dreamt its truth.

Before you get too far along in your thinking about conclusive signs of wakefulness, it is worth noting that the sceptic has a ready reply for any of them. She can say that you have just dreamt the sign. Suppose you say that waking life is ordered, clear, vivid or whatever. The sceptic can say that dreams can sometimes be ordered, clear, vivid, and so on. Maybe you think that you can tell the difference between dreams and waking life because you always wake up after a dream and then you can tell the difference. The sceptic can point to false awakenings, instances in which one dreams that one has just woken up. It goes without saying that you can dream a pinch on the arm too.

Descartes thinks the argument from dreams proves quite a bit. However, he thinks that the images we experience while dreaming are like paintings which can only be formed from something real. When a painter paints a unicorn, for example, he has in mind something real, namely horses and horns, and combines them. Dreaming experiences have to come from something real too, but here Descartes exercises the caution required of the method of doubt. Maybe general things like hands and fires do not really exist, but there might be more simple and universal entities. He concludes that aspects of corporeal nature as such – figure, quantity, size, number, place and time in general – really exist, but beliefs about particular things are now suspect. He therefore rejects beliefs attending the study of physics, astronomy and medicine – in short, any beliefs which depend on composite entities. Only beliefs which do not depend on the real existence of particular things, such as those about maths and logic, remain.

Descartes casts doubt on these remaining beliefs by considering his origin. Either he was created by an all-powerful God or by some lesser mechanism, perhaps a random series of accidents. If God made him, then it is certainly possible that such a being could have constructed him in such a way that even his beliefs about maths and logic are false. He might be built so as to think triangles have four sides. If he owes his origin to something less than God, maybe a fortuitous series of accidental causes, then it is even more likely that he has some design flaws. Either way, he has reason to doubt his capacity to form true beliefs about even the most simple and universal things.

At the conclusion of this argument, he writes: 'I have certainly nothing to say in reply to such reasonings, but am constrained to avow that, of all the opinions that I once accepted as true, there is not one which is not now legitimately open to doubt.' To keep this stark conclusion in view, he employs a psychological device, the so-called 'Evil Demon'. He has a little difficulty, he says, in thinking that God might deceive him, so instead he imagines a malicious demon, as powerful and cunning as he is treacherous, who is occupied entirely with deceiving him. This, in conjunction with the three arguments above, seems to leave Descartes in doubt of all his beliefs.

The Cogito

But there is one belief, one hardy proposition, which he simply cannot doubt. If he is deceived by his senses, if he is lost in a dream, if his origins are such that he is a faulty thinker, even if a vicious demon is bent on his confusion, it still remains beyond doubt that he exists. As Descartes puts it: '*I am, I exist*, is necessarily true, every time I express it or conceive of it in my mind.' We have here not only a version of the most famous philosophical catchphrase ever written, but also the first truth, the foundation upon which Descartes rebuilds his system of knowledge. This first truth is sometimes called 'the Cogito', shorthand for the Latin expression '*Cogito ergo sum*'; 'I think, therefore I am'.

The status of the Cogito has occupied philosophers ever since. Numerous questions about it arise almost instantly. Is it the conclusion of an argument? It is not clear that it could be, as Descartes has admitted that he has no beliefs, no premises with which to construct an argument. Anyway, he has also said that he has no faith in his capacity to construct arguments, no trust in logic. Some therefore view the Cogito not as the conclusion of an argument but as a kind of epistemic discovery: an indubitable truth he stumbles upon. Others worry about whether or not he is entitled to the 'I' in the Cogito. Isn't he entitled only to something far less, perhaps just that thinking occurs, rather than that the thinker is Descartes himself?

Cartesian Dualism

Leave this aside for the time being and follow Descartes a little further. He knows that he exists, but asks what sort of thing he is. Before he considered the three sceptical arguments above, he thought he was a man: both flesh and bones and a mind which thinks. Now, he maintains, strictly speaking he is only sure that he is a thinking thing – a thing which doubts, affirms, wills, seems to see, and so on. He is no longer sure that he has hands or a body at all. But if he can doubt that he has a body while remaining certain that he has a mind, are not the mind and body distinct things?

This is the nugget of Cartesian Dualism, the view that the mind and body are different substances, and the line of thought which leads to it is sometimes called the conceivability argument for dualism. I can conceive of my mind and body existing separately; Descartes has imagined just this in the first meditation. If it is conceivable that mind and body are different things, then it is possible that they are different things. If this is possible, then mind and body cannot be identical. You can try to talk yourself into this view by thinking of other identities. Can you, for example, imagine water existing without H_2O existing? You probably can't, because they are the same thing. However, we certainly can conceive of mind and body coming apart, of one existing without the other, and Descartes' point is that we would not be able to do that if mind and body were identical. You can talk yourself out of this view, as many have done, by noting that conceivability is no guide to metaphysical possibility. Conceivability tells us something about the concepts we use to think about the world but says nothing about how the world really is.

Cartesian Dualism, then, is the view that the universe has two different kinds of stuff in it. It has mind in it, stuff which thinks and is not spatially located, and it has body in it, stuff which occupies space. The largest objection to this version of dualism is the problem of interaction. We know that mind and body seem to stand in causal relation. Stub your toe and your mind registers pain; think about making a fist and your body should be able to accommodate you. But how are we to understand the fact of such everyday interactions when mind and body, on Descartes' view, are such different things? How can something which is not in space, the mind, stand in a causal relationship to something which is in space, the body? Mind–body interaction is just a mystery for the dualist, and contemporary philosophy of mind can be viewed as an attempt to think ourselves out of this mystery. It is not clear that we have made much headway.

The Cartesian circle

Descartes tries to make headway, though, by looking for further truths in the contents of his mind. He thinks a little about the nature of doubt, and reasons that doubting is a kind of imperfection, as compared to knowing. Reflection on the very idea of perfection leads him to one of several proofs of the existence of God. Descartes knows, given the nature of his various doubts, that he is not a perfect being. Nevertheless, he has the idea of perfection, and such an idea could not have come from him or any other imperfect being. It could only come from a perfect being, namely God. The line of thought leads to a version of Anselm's ontological proof. The idea Descartes has of God is of a being with all perfections. Existence is a kind of perfection, so God must exist. Thinking of God as not existing is like trying to think of a triangle without three sides. Just as three-sidedness is in the concept of triangularity, existence is in the concept of God. If you really understand the idea of God, you have to accept that God exists.

Deception, Descartes notes, is a kind of imperfection, so he reasons that God must be no deceiver. Therefore we can have confidence in our clear and distinct perceptions, we are not systematically misled, and truth is something we must be equipped to find. Rebuilding a system of belief rooted in clear and distinct perception is the business of the remainder of the meditations.

Many have noticed a very tight circle in this line of argument. We come to know that God exists and is no deceiver by assenting only to a series of clear and distinct perceptions. We know that our clear and distinct perceptions are trustworthy because God exists and is no deceiver. But doesn't our faith in clear and distinct perceptions depend on the proof that God is no deceiver, and doesn't that proof presuppose the veracity of our clear and distinct perceptions?

The trouble here, and perhaps with the *Meditations* generally, is that knowledge seems a fragile thing. Descartes certainly seems to succeed in the negative part of his project, razing the foundations of knowledge with the sceptical arguments of the first meditation. His effort to build everything up from nothing, however, is a kind of failure. But his general aim, to show that a scientific understanding of the universe is possible, is something we moderns take to easily. You can try to explain this by thinking about our distance from the intellectual upheavals of Descartes' day. Whatever your explanation of this fact, it will not be complete without some mention of Descartes himself.

5 Leviathan
Thomas Hobbes (1588–1679)

According to a story which many make a little too much of, Hobbes was born prematurely when his mother was frightened into an early labour on hearing the news that the Spanish Armada was approaching. 'Fear and I were born twins,' he said. Certainly fear plays a central role in Hobbes' great work, *Leviathan*, but whether this is owed to Hobbes' psychology or human psychology generally is another matter. We will leave it to the biographers.

What is clear, though, is that *Leviathan* marks a break with virtually all of the thinking about politics which came before it, thinking which depends on religious considerations. Some maintain that Hobbes was a covert atheist. In fact, Parliament investigated the possibility that London's Great Fire was divine retribution for Hobbes' blasphemous writings. They thought that Hobbes might have irritated God and actually insisted, just to be on the safe side, that he stop publishing. In any case, it is true that his conception of political obligation is rooted not in divine will, but in reason. This is not to say that religion is ignored in the book: large parts of it are devoted to the theological justification of conclusions reached elsewhere. But scriptural authority takes a back seat to rationality in *Leviathan*, and recognizable political philosophy comes into the world in its pages.

Like Descartes, Hobbes was much influenced by mathematics. Instead of following Descartes and applying the formal rules of mathematical proof to thinking generally, Hobbes focused on the role of definition in geometry. By setting out the proper definitions of such words as 'sense', 'imagination', 'desire', 'right' and 'law', he hoped to come to true conclusions about them. We give names to our thoughts, he maintains, and thinking about those thoughts is a kind of mental arithmetic, the addition and subtraction of thoughts through carefully defined terms. Beginning with proper definitions and following the consequences through to the truth is Hobbes' method.

Again like Descartes, Hobbes was influenced by Galileo and the general view of the universe as fundamentally mechanistic. Hobbes, though, had little time for incorporeal substance. He takes it that the universe itself is matter in motion in space, a kind of clockwork engine. The same can be said of its parts, including animals and human beings: all are machines in motion. Appetite or desire is just motion towards some object, and aversion or fear is just motion away from some object. The introduction to *Leviathan* places the mechanical view of human beings at the centre of Hobbes' thinking. He begins the book by arguing that life is a kind of mechanized motion of limbs – the heart is a spring, the nerves are strings, and the joints are wheels. The state is an artificial person no less mechanistic in nature than an ordinary person – the judiciary is its joints, a system of rewards and punishments are its nerves, and what actuates the whole is its sovereign.

As Galileo demonstrated, we can formulate general statements about the motion of matter in the universe. The mechanistic view of human beings and their political organization holds out a kind of promise of the discovery of natural laws of human psychology and, on a larger scale, the origin of commonwealths too. The discovery of the natural laws underpinning political obligation is the goal of *Leviathan*. Hobbes approaches these laws in particular and political obligation in general by reflection on the state of nature, an image of ungoverned human beings. What he discovers is by no means uplifting. It depends on a depressing conception of human nature.

The state of nature

Before we come to it, though, we will put one worry aside. It is worth wondering how best to understand the state of nature, and one answer gets more than its share of attention. Some literalists maintain that Hobbes is actually theorizing that something like the state of nature really existed, that human beings once lived ungoverned, running amok until some bright spark managed to write up a social contract and collect signatures. They rightly conclude that if Hobbes is speculating about human prehistory, he is guilty of oversimplification at the very least. But Hobbes need not commit himself to any of this. He might claim that talk of the state of nature is a conceptual exercise, not an historical one. He is trying to uncover the justification of political obligation by considering what human life might be like in its absence. The question of whether or not the state of nature really existed is beside the point.

In the state of nature, Hobbes maintains that human beings have a certain measure of dark equality. Like the steps of a geometrical proof, three facts about human psychology follow quickly from this. We are all more or less equal in physical strength and faculties of the mind, and here Hobbes notes that this amounts to a kind of equality of insecurity. Anyone has the capacity to kill anyone else, either alone or by forming a temporary alliance with others. Everyone lacking government is in the same kind of danger and shares the same sort of fear for his life. The first component of the psychology of a person in the state of nature is, therefore, diffidence or fear.

The second component has to do with want and competition. Hobbes imagines that resources are limited, if not scarce, and human beings are bound to need the same sorts of things. Given the natural equality of everyone in the state of nature, everyone has a kind of equal claim to whatever she wants, and there is no obvious way to settle disputes, except by force. Human beings, for Hobbes, naturally fall into a kind of general struggle for things in the world.

Third, and finally, humans have a natural desire for glory. This also can follow from the natural equality characteristic of humans in the state of nature. If no one is better than anyone else, then being undervalued is a kind of affront, which humans are quick to notice. It can result in taking offence very quickly. In us is also a desire to win the approval of our fellows, or perhaps just incite fear in those against us. However we characterize it, the desire for glory is a cause of further suffering in the state of nature.

Hobbes is describing a general state of war, but the struggle is between individuals and not states: a war of 'every man against every man'. In this condition, there can be no industry, culture, navigation, architecture, knowledge, arts or society. In the absence of these – the satisfactions of civilization – there is only fear. Further, as there is no government, there are no laws to break. So, Hobbes thinks, there can be no justice, no such thing as right or wrong, and no property. Everyone has an equal right to everything and an equal right to do whatever is necessary to protect and preserve himself. You would not enjoy life in the state of nature, but you might take some comfort in the knowledge that you would not last very long. As Hobbes famously put it, life in the state of nature is 'solitary, poor, nasty, brutish, and short'.

Laws of Nature

If there is a ray of light in this murky conception of humanity, it is that human beings would not revel in the state of nature. If left to our own devices, we would naturally fall into something horrible, but it is also true that we naturally want to get ourselves out of it. Hobbes maintains that two forces, passion and reason, are responsible for our flight from the state of nature. What nudges us in the direction of peace is a general fear of death and insecurity, a desire for a decent life, and a kind of inbuilt hope for it. What secures the path to peace, though, is reason. Hobbes draws up a large list of laws of nature – rules or dictates of reason, in other words – which any rational person should find binding. The first law seems to follow from both our nature and the general awfulness of the state of nature as Hobbes describes it. The rest might be seen as consequences of the first law, dictates which we must accept if we accept the first.

The first law of nature is this: 'every man ought to endeavour peace, as far as he has hope of obtaining it; and when he cannot obtain it, that he may seek and use all helps and advantages of war'. The first part of the law, that everyone ought to seek peace, follows from the fact that staying in the state of nature is dangerous, harmful to one. It is therefore rational to want to get out of it. The second part is an expression of what Hobbes calls 'the sum of the right of nature', a general right we all have to defend ourselves. Seeking the peace, then, is the most rational means of self-defence presented to someone in the state of nature.

The second law is a necessary consequence of the first: 'that a man be willing, when others are so too, as far forth as for peace and defense of himself he shall think it necessary, to lay down this right to all things, and be contented with so much liberty against other men, as he would allow men against himself'. The general condition of war characteristic of the state of nature depends on everyone having a kind of universal liberty, a right to everything. If seeking the peace is rationally required, then this general right must be forfeited. Rationality requires, however, that you give up only so much as others have given up. Otherwise, you are prey, as good a victim as you might have been in the state of nature.

The voluntary and mutual transferral of a right Hobbes calls a 'contract'. If a person gives something up and leaves the other con-tractor to do the same on trust, the contract becomes a 'covenant'. The third law of nature is that we must stick to our contracts and covenants, otherwise, again, we will never get ourselves out of the state of nature. Further laws of nature follow, which instruct us to be just, equitable, modest, merciful and, in an echo of biblical teaching, generally do unto others as we would have them do unto us.

The Leviathan

It might be comforting to read Hobbes as arguing that human reason bootstraps us out of the aspects of human nature which led us to the state of nature in the first place. The unpleasantness is something we put aside once reason is given its head; once the laws of nature are before us, we all consent to give up our natural right to everything, keep our contracts with one another, and go about our happy, civilized business. For Hobbes, it is not so. Our natural passions – partiality, pride, revenge, and so on – eventually overcome rational injunctions to be just, modest and to follow the Golden Rule. We are not to be trusted. Contracts are nothing without fear of what might happen to us if we break them. As Hobbes puts it, 'covenants, without the sword, are but words'.

The sword which renders the social contract binding is a 'common power', the result of every individual giving up his or her liberty, power and strength to one person or assembly, on the condition that everyone else gives up everything too. The social contract, then, requires the voluntary and mutual transferral of individual rights and powers to a single entity, the head of state or parliamentary assembly. Hobbes' characterization is unrestrained: 'This is the generation of that great LEVIATHAN, or rather, to speak more reverently, of that *mortal God*, to which we owe under the *immortal God*, our peace and defence.'

A number of facts follow from all of this, according to Hobbes. First of all, because the subjects contract to confer their power on the sovereign, the sovereign is not a party to the contract. There is then no sense in which he can break the contract, no sense in which he is contractually obliged to do anything, and no way for him to do something which might get the people out of the contract. The king's power is in no sense conditional. Hobbes suggests elsewhere, in a consideration of 'free gifts', that reason demands that he avoid ingratitude, that the people have no reasonable cause to think better of handing him the mantle, but this is scarcely a curb on governmental power.

Hobbes also argues that those who might wish to dissent from the contract must now go along with the crowd, for two reasons. First, if the dissenters bail out of the contract when things are not going as they might have wished, their late departure indicates tacit consent further upstream. The notion of tacit consent is as old as Socrates, who argued that one had an obligation to obey all the laws of the city, not just the convenient ones, because by staying under the city's protection, one gives a kind of unspoken consent to be governed. Second, dissenters who insist on opting out of the contract will find themselves back in the state of nature, a clear target for anyone who cares to take aim. Rationality requires that they consent.

There is also a sense, Hobbes insists, in which the king can never be unjust or thought of as injuring his subjects. Strictly speaking, everyone who contracts together creates the sovereign, and so any action undertaken by the sovereign is ultimately rooted in that original act. The king acts as a result of the previous actions of the subjects, so a subject has no just cause to complain about the king's actions. The king's actions depend on the prior actions of the subjects, namely their contracting together with everyone else.

Difficulties for absolutism

By now you might be thinking that something has gone wrong in Hobbes' conception of political obligation, and your objections probably have something to do with its absolute nature. According to Hobbes, there is no sense in which the government can enact an unjust law or do something morally wrong. Justice and injustice, right and wrong, are only given meaning by the state itself, only come into existence when the leviathan is born. You can think of counter-examples in the form of unjust laws and morally wrong governmental practices. It is easy to wonder whether Hobbes really is committed to the view that, say, the Civil Rights Movement in America was itself wrong or unjust, or that civil disobedience generally is always wrong, or that the overthrow of a government is never morally acceptable. It is possible to object, too, on the grounds that some higher conception of justice or morality exists, something other than the mere dictates of a state.

Something might have gone wrong, too, in Hobbes' claim that the fear we might have of the state of nature can lead us to empower someone who not only stands a chance of ensuring peace, but also claims supreme and unlimited authority. Is it rational to flee your fellows by embracing something even more dangerous, namely the absolute power of a monarch? As Locke asks, a little incredulously, 'Are men so foolish that they take care to avoid what mischiefs may be done them by polecats or foxes, but are content, nay think it safety, to be devoured by lions?'

Perhaps the problem is further upstream, somewhere in Hobbes' conception of human nature. Maybe we are not so awful to one another after all, at least not so awful as to require an absolute power to keep us from killing one another. If Hobbes has mischaracterized human nature, the demand for an absolute government has much less force. Maybe Hobbes' emphasis on the worst in us has something to do with the possibly undue influence of the events of Hobbes' time on his thinking. He knew something of the horrors of the Civil War, and he might have thought that anything, even absolutism, was preferable to something so terrible.

Many have rejected Hobbes' absolutist conclusions, on more grounds than those scouted above. Still, even contemporary talk of political obligation owes much to Hobbes' conception of the social contract. His break with the view that governmental authority depends somehow on divine authority has been followed both by philosophers and by those who actually have a hand in governmental decision making. By some lights, it is a straight line from Hobbes' revolution in political thinking to the revolutions in America, France and elsewhere.

6 An Essay Concerning Human Understanding
John Locke (1632–1704)

Some people stay up late at night, perhaps with a drink or two, arguing about what truth there is in politics, morality and religion. Such people can be at loggerheads, and sometimes the argument is partly resolved with the realization that the disputing parties just have different beliefs about what can be known. What most people don't do after such a conversation, and what Locke in fact did, is spend the better part of the following 20 years delineating the origins, extent and conditions of knowledge. The result was *An Essay Concerning Human Understanding*, and philosophy changed with its publication.

The change consists in a departure from rationalism, a family of views which bases human knowledge on reason or rational intuition, as opposed to sensory experience. Rationalism has roots in pre-Socratic thinking, but it was no doubt Plato's philosophy which had the largest influence on Locke's predecessors. For Plato, knowledge is permanent – something known today cannot become false tomorrow. However, the senses can only give us momentarily true opinions about the changing world of experience. The senses can tell us 'it's raining', but eventually it won't be raining, and that sentence will be false. Knowledge, though, is permanent. If we know '2 + 2 = 4', we have a handle on something which will stay true, no matter what might happen with the weather.

If we really do know anything, for Plato, it is reason which delivers the goods. If sensation cannot help us in our efforts to know, we must be born with all we need to know what we actually do know. Plato, of course, noticed that not everyone has an equal share in knowledge; certainly children are not born with much in the way of it. Plato argues that we acquire knowledge before birth, by visiting an unchanging world of conceptual realities. We know what beauty is, for example, by beholding the Beautiful itself. We forget all this during birth, but we stand a chance of recalling it through philosophical enquiry.

It is an extravagant solution to a difficult problem, but you can take Plato's point without committing yourself to the rest of it. What particular sensory experience or set of experiences could tell us that the whole is greater than its parts, that no self-contradiction is true, that murder is wrong, or that God exists? If everyone claims to know some or all of this, and sensation is no help, why not suppose that we are all born with such truths imprinted on our minds?

Locke's *Essay* answers this question, first by attacking rationalist arguments for the notion that some ideas are innate, which is the business of book one. Book two sets up the alternative, empiricism, with a consideration of ideas, their origins and nature. Book three is concerned with words and language, and of particular importance is Locke's treatment of 'substance' and 'essence'. Book four deals with the scope of knowledge and the nature of certainty.

You should brace yourself for the fact that it is impossible to understand Locke's views without working your way through a large number of distinctions – distinctions between ideas of sense and reflection, simple and complex ideas, primary and secondary qualities, degrees of certainty, and so on. The many distinctions are just a feature of Locke's writing and thinking. Console yourself with the fact that once you have a grip on Locke's distinctions, you are on your way to understanding a large chunk of philosophy. The pay-off is well worth it.

Locke's project has two sorts of overall aims. First, he claims that before we spend the night arguing about morality and politics, we must first 'examine our own abilities, and see what *objects* our understandings [are, or are not] fitted to deal with'. Locke is doing 'first philosophy' in Descartes' sense; he is putting epistemology at the heart of philosophical enquiry. By determining what it is we are capable of knowing, we can direct our attention properly, focus our faculties where they might do some good and rest quietly when we have no hope of understanding something. Second, he is defending the philosophical underpinnings of the empiricist methods of contemporaries such as Newton and Boyle. In a rhetorical flourish, Locke claims to be 'clearing Ground a little, and removing some of the Rubbish, that lies in the way of knowledge'. He is tidying up philosophy, and the first thing to go is the doctrine of innate ideas.

Innate ideas

Locke maintains that defenders of the doctrine of innate ideas have one argument: the argument from general assent. Rationalists point to certain principles, for example: 'what is, is'; and 'it is impossible for the same thing to be and not be'. The claim is that such principles are universally agreed upon by everyone – everyone accepts them, and no one denies them. The rationalist claims that this universal agreement is explained by the fact that such principles or ideas are innate: we are all just born with them.

Locke's flat response has two parts. First of all, he claims that universal agreement does not prove that the ideas in question are innate. Even if there are some principles which everyone or nearly everyone accepts, there might be some explanation other than the existence of innate ideas. The other explanation is offered elsewhere in the book, where Locke maintains that agreement can be explained from the empirical point of view. Second, and perhaps more importantly, Locke argues that there really are no principles to which everyone assents. 'Children and idiots', he says, cannot even apprehend the principles in question, let alone assent to them.

Empiricism

Whether or not you find this convincing, the real work against rationalism begins in the second book of the *Essay*, where Locke outlines his alternative to it. The empirical view begins with Locke's account of ideas, which he defines as 'whatsoever is the *object* of the understanding when a man thinks'. Suppose Locke is right and that there are no innate ideas – the mind is a blank slate (a *tabula rasa*) at birth. Where, then, do ideas come from? Locke's answer is experience.

He argues that experience itself is of just two types. When our eyes, ears, noses, fingers and tongues are affected by physical objects, our minds are furnished with ideas of sensible objects. When our minds reflect on the ideas they have from sensation – when we think, doubt, believe, reason, know, will, and so on – when we experience this activity, our minds are furnished with ideas of reflection. All ideas without exception, Locke argues, come from these two sources. Encountering sensible objects provides the understanding with ideas of sensation, and a consideration of the operations of the mind itself provides the understanding with ideas of reflection.

If he does not provide a proof of this claim about the origins of our ideas, he does offer a few considerations in support of it. Locke suggests, first, that you analyse your own store of ideas, daring you to point to one which does not arise either from sensation or reflection. He also returns to a consideration of children, arguing that the cumulative way in which a child learns fits the empirical theory much better than the doctrine of innate ideas. Children seem born with little in the way of understanding, and what they do eventually understand is a function of what they experience. Finally, he notes that people have different ideas, and this seems to depend on the objects they encounter. If you have never paid much attention to a clock, spent no time examining its parts, you will not have many ideas about one. You certainly will have nothing like the ideas in the head of the experienced watchmaker. All of this, Locke thinks, should nudge you in the direction of empiricism.

Ideas and qualities

Once the proposition that ideas originate in experience has been established, Locke maintains that a close look at the nature of ideas themselves is in order. He argues that all ideas generally are of two types: simple and complex. A simple idea is 'nothing but *one uniform appearance or conception in the mind*, and is not distinguishable into different ideas'. Simple ideas have no parts, but complex ideas are themselves built up of simple ideas. Although our experience of, say, a rose is in a sense blended – what we experience when we examine a rose is a complex bundle of sensory ideas – we have no difficulty in separating out the simple ideas of red, the distinctive smell of a rose, the feel of the petals, and so on. Each of these simple ideas cannot be further reduced to still more simple ideas. The smell of a rose has no parts.

Simple ideas have another important property: the mind can neither create nor destroy them. Once simple ideas have been imprinted on the mind, the mind has the power to re-create them, call them up in the imagination, compare them, even create new complex ideas by combining various simple ideas in novel ways. What the mind cannot do, though, is generate simple ideas without first experiencing the objects which give rise to them. If you have never experienced the particular properties of drunkenness, you will have to wait until you have experienced enough beer.

What, then, is the relation between our ideas and the properties of objects in the world? Locke calls the power of an object to produce ideas in us its 'qualities'. Locke makes a distinction between the primary and secondary qualities of objects. Primary qualities are 'utterly inseparable' from the objects themselves, no matter what might happen to the objects in question. A piece of paper has solidity, extension, figure, mobility and number. Tear it in half or shred it into a thousand pieces, and the pieces themselves, still have those same qualities. So when we have ideas of primary qualities, our ideas really resemble the properties of the objects we are experiencing.

Secondary qualities, though, are 'nothing in the objects themselves, but powers to produce various sensations in us by their primary qualities'. Locke has in mind colours, sounds, tastes, and so on. The brick wall I can see from my window really has the quality of solidity, but its dappled colours are not really in the wall at all. The colours, like all secondary qualities, depend on my sensory apparatus. Its solidity, though, does not. Take all the perceivers out of the world, and the secondary qualities vanish, while, Locke maintains, the primary qualities remain.

Knowledge

Locke reaches a number of conclusions based on just this consideration of the nature of ideas. Ideas are real, Locke argues, when they have a foundation in the physical world. Given his account of simple ideas, there is a sense in which all simple ideas are real; the mind cannot just generate them, so they must come from the world itself. You can prove a part of this to yourself by trying to imagine an entirely new primary colour. (I tend to manage only a variation on brown.)

However, saying that an idea is real is not to say that it is an adequate representation of the qualities of objects. Some ideas, namely the ideas we have of secondary qualities, might be real in Locke's sense, but they are not really in the objects which cause them. They therefore cannot represent anything in the world. Our simple ideas of primary qualities, however, really do represent actual qualities in objects, or so Locke maintains.

You can start wondering, as Berkeley and Hume did, how Locke could know that the ideas we have of primary qualities really represent the properties of the things in the world. Note that Locke claims that the objects of human understanding are ideas, not physical objects. On his view we only know about physical objects indirectly, via our direct acquaintance with ideas. If this is so, then there seems no way at all to compare our ideas of the qualities of objects with the qualities of objects themselves. We seem trapped in a mental prison of ideas. If you take this part of empiricism very seriously, it can lead quickly to scepticism. We will come to this in our consideration of later empiricists. Locke, though, does not succumb to scepticism, at least not a general scepticism. He insists that there is much that we can know, certainly enough to get about the business of living.

Since ideas are the only objects of human understanding, knowledge, for Locke, is 'nothing but the perception of the connexion and agreement, or disagreement and repugnancy, of any of our ideas'. This agreement or disagreement comes in four flavours: identity and diversity; relation; co-existence or necessary connection; and real existence. We can know that ideas are the same or different, that they are related in some way, that they always exist together, or that they correspond to something which exists outside the mind.

Consider identity and diversity. Locke argues that when we perceive any idea, there is a kind of brute knowledge that the idea in question is what it is, and also a corresponding brute knowledge that the idea in question is not something else. We know that white is white (identity), and that white is not black (diversity). Without this bare recognition, we would never be able to tell the difference between different ideas or recognize the reappearance of an idea. Is this a capitulation to the rationalist claim that there is an innate idea lurking here – that 'what is, is' is with us from birth? Not at all. Locke is arguing that we perceive identity and diversity in particular ideas, without recourse to some general, innate principle. No such principle, Locke claims, could make the bare facts of identity and diversity more certain to us than they already are. We have no need of innate principles.

Given his outline of the nature of knowledge as agreement or disagreement, Locke identifies three sorts of knowledge: intuitive, demonstrative and sensitive. Intuitive knowledge – for example, my knowledge that white is white – is the most certain sort of knowledge. Demonstrative knowledge – say, the knowledge which comes at the end of a mathematical proof – is less certain. The mind might not be able to grasp the agreement between two ideas immediately, as it can in the case of intuition, but through a series of intervening intuitions, a demonstration, we can come to see the connections between ideas. Less certain but still a kind of knowledge is sensitive knowledge – for example, my knowledge that this particular pencil exists. There is a difference between seeing a sunset and just picturing it in the mind, being in a fire and thinking about being in a fire. Locke claims that there is a kind of sensory evidence which puts us past doubting the existence of some particular objects. It carries with it nothing like the certainty which attends intuition or even demonstration, but still, he claims, sensation brings with it more than mere probability.

All of this leads to a series of conclusions about the scope and limits of human knowledge, and it leaves us with only a feeble grip on the things in the world. As the immediate objects of our understanding are ideas, our knowledge can only go as far as our ideas go. In fact, as we can never come to know all the relations that ideas have with one another, our knowledge does not even go as far as our ideas. Our ideas, anyway, are for Locke imperfect windows on the world. We can know that our ideas are representative of the primary qualities of objects, but the ideas we have of secondary qualities are not in the objects themselves. Why objects cause the secondary qualities they do is beyond us too. Further, although we can notice that ideas always co-exist or stand in necessary connections, we can never come to know why this is so. We are, Locke claims, cut off from knowing about the real existence and nature of things, and this, he says, prevents us from developing a certain science of physical objects. We have intuitive knowledge of our own existence, demonstrative knowledge, for example, that God exists, and sensitive knowledge that there are things in the world, but pressing our knowledge of those things into perfect focus is beyond our ken.

It is possible to have the feeling that something is missing from Locke's claim that sensory experience generates a kind of knowledge. How do we know that there really is a sunset or a fire, if all we have are ideas of sunsets and fires? You can also begin to wonder, as Leibniz did, if we really can do without innate ideas. Experience only gives us examples, particular truths at best, but we seem to know general truths too. My senses can tell me that all the snails I have seen eat lettuce, but what gets me to the conclusion that all snails eat lettuce? Don't I need some innate principles to carry me from individual truths to general ones? These worries pepper Locke's work, and they occupy the philosophers who follow him. Without question, though, philosophy has taken up Locke's empiricism, worries and all.

7 A Treatise Concerning the Principles of Human Knowledge
George Berkeley (1685–1753)

Who says philosophy is merely an armchair discipline, with no grounding in scientific experimentation? Here is an experiment you can undertake in the privacy of your own home, right now, which might prove to you the philosophical thesis that there is a distinction between appearance and reality. Fix your gaze on some object, then stick a finger in your eye just hard enough to double your vision. What is it, exactly, which just doubled? You can say, preposterously, that the act of sticking a finger in your eye results in the physical object you are observing literally doubling for a moment. Or you can say that the object did not really double. What doubled was a mental image, a representation of the object. What doubled was an appearance in your head; the reality out there remained unchanged.

If you are willing to go along with this distinction, you can start to wonder about the relation between your mental representations and the objects in the world. What we are in direct or immediate contact with – the objects of human understanding, as Locke would have it – are mental images. Through our mental images, then, we are only indirectly aware of the things in the world. It does not take much in the way of a sceptical turn of mind to wonder how we know that our mental representations really represent the things in the world. When I see a cabbage, what I am directly aware of is a mental image. How do I know that my mental image really represents the cabbage as it is, out there in the world? I cannot climb out of my head and compare the image and the cabbage itself – all I have to work with are the images. You can push the boat out a little and wonder how anyone could possibly know that there really are cabbages out there at all.

There are a number of answers to this brand of scepticism, but perhaps the most astonishing one appears in Berkeley's *A Treatise*

Concerning the Principles of Human Knowledge. There is no room for scepticism in Berkeley's universe, because there is no question of our mental images standing in relation to something physical outside our heads. To put it starkly, Berkeley argues that only minds and the ideas in them exist.

In arguing for this claim, Berkeley does two things. First of all, he aims to refute scepticism and defend common sense. It is his view that scepticism about external objects becomes possible once we entertain a distinction between the experienced properties of objects and the objects as they are, independent of experience. When philosophers came round to the view that there exists some material substratum – some something, we know not what – which underpins our experiences, Berkeley argues that the confusions which resulted lead only to scepticism. '[W]e have first raised a dust and then complain we cannot see.' Berkeley hopes to return us to clear thinking by eliminating some of the dust, namely, the notion of physical substance or matter. Second, Berkeley is reacting to materialism and the atheism he believes is inherent in it. By placing God, not matter, at the centre of things, Berkeley is, in a sense, making religion and morality possible again.

The book itself was largely ignored in Berkeley's lifetime, and many who actually did read it took it as an example of the foolish excesses of philosophical speculation. Dr Samuel Johnson allegedly amused himself and others by kicking a stone and saying: 'I refute him thus.'

Berkeley tried again with *Three Dialogues Between Hylas and Philonous*, which patiently guides the reader through his arguments in dialogue form, dealing with the most obvious objections to the view along the way. This book was also overlooked in Berkeley's day. Both books, though, have many virtues. Berkeley is nothing if not a clear and engaging writer, and the *Principles* is well structured and easy to follow. The central argument of the book emerges in just the first six paragraphs, with the remainder of the principles devoted primarily to dealing with objections and clarifying his arguments.

The argument for idealism

Berkeley begins with a consideration of abstract ideas, and then offers three plain claims about ideas and minds. His conclusion, the truth of subjective idealism or the view that only minds and the ideas in them exist, follows quickly. He then deals with objections to his position and runs some interesting arguments for the existence of God, the nature of perception and science, and the immortality of the soul. We will have a look at some of this in what follows.

Berkeley's first plain claim is this: the objects of human knowledge are ideas. Ideas themselves are of three types, on Berkeley's view. There are ideas imprinted on the mind through sensory experience; ideas formed by introspectively noting the passions and operations of the mind; and ideas called up by memory or the imagination. The second plain claim is this: in addition to ideas, 'there is likewise something which knows or perceives them; and exercises diverse operations, as willing, imagining, remembering, about them. This perceiving, active being is what I call *mind, spirit, soul* or *myself'*. Minds, in other words, are the perceivers of ideas. The third plain claim is this: the existence of an idea consists in being perceived.

It is worth pausing over the third claim for a moment. Ideas can exist only in a mind which perceives them. My coffee has a certain smell, a bitter taste, a shade of brown, a fading warmth, and so on. Smells cannot exist unsmelled, tastes cannot exist untasted, colours have to be seen, and warmth is what it is only when felt. Smells, tastes and the like require smellers and tasters, minds to perceive them. For ideas, Berkeley insists, *esse est percipi*: to be is to be perceived. Their existence depends entirely on perceivers.

Sensory ideas – like colours, shapes and sounds – are 'observed to accompany each other'. A certain version of red, a sweet taste, a particular smell, a round shape, and maybe a crunchy sound accompany each other in a regular set of sensory ideas we call an 'apple'. The mind easily thinks of this collection as a single thing. But philosophers take an additional step and suppose that the thing has existence outside of a perceiving mind. Berkeley's objection is to this additional step.

He argues that the claim that the apple exists unperceived is a manifest contradiction. What are objects 'but the things we perceive by sense? and what do we perceive *besides our own ideas or sensations?* and is it not plainly repugnant that any of these, or any combination of them, should exist unperceived?' The apple, the coffee, the desk, the wall, this carpet – all of the things I am currently perceiving – are collections of tastes, smells, sights, sounds and feels. Such things can only exist in a perceiving mind. How could the taste of this coffee exist unless someone tasted it? To suppose that tastes could exist untasted is to involve oneself in a contradiction. It is to suppose that perceptions can exist unperceived and, for Berkeley, this makes no sense at all.

Objections and Berkeley's replies

You might be thinking that something has gone very wrong here. Of course perceptions cannot exist unperceived, but perceptions are perceptions of real objects, which exist whether we perceive them or not. Our perceptions are in our heads, certainly, but the objects our perceptions represent, the things in the world, can and do exist mind-independently. There is no manifest contradiction in supposing that our perceptions represent things that exist unperceived.

What you are proposing is a version of representative realism, and Berkeley has a ready reply for you. The representative realist claims that inner representations are somehow like physical objects. My mental image of Cameron the horse, say, has certain properties: horsey smells, feels, sounds, and so on. The real Cameron out there in the material field might not have exactly this set of properties. Still, the properties of the mental image represent the properties of the real horse. My equine mental image is like the real thing – maybe it is like the real horse in the same way a photocopy is like an original document, a photo of a sunset is like a real sunset, and so on.

Berkeley argues that this makes no sense at all. How can an idea be like anything other than another idea? How could a smell be like something which has no smell? How could the way something feels represent something we cannot feel at all? All we feel are the feels, not the properties those feels allegedly represent. If the horse-in-the-world is directly perceivable, then it is a set of ideas existing in your mind, and Berkeley is happy that you finally agree with him. But if you think the horse-in-the-world is not directly perceivable, that you know the real thing only through mental properties which somehow represent the horse-in-the-world, then you have some explaining to do. Can perceptions really represent something which we do not perceive? Berkeley, a little exasperated, says: 'I appeal to anyone whether it be sense to assert that a colour is like something which is invisible; hard or soft, like something which is intangible; and so of the rest.'

You can try again by appealing to Locke's distinction between primary and secondary qualities. As we have seen, Locke argues that our ideas of the primary qualities of objects – extension, figure, motion, solidity and number – are 'utterly inseparable' from the objects themselves. However, our ideas of secondary qualities – tastes, smells, sounds, feels, colours and the like – are nothing in the objects themselves but powers to produce various sensations in us. You can argue that Berkeley is talking about secondary qualities only. His claim is that the properties of objects are nothing but mind-dependent properties, but the properties he mentions are just the secondary ones. We knew this already; we knew that secondary qualities are mind-dependent, not really out there in any robust sense. However, objects really do have primary qualities, whether we perceive them or not. The primary qualities are in matter, and we really can have ideas of them through sensation.

Again, Berkeley has a reply. The student of Locke will readily admit that the secondary qualities of objects exist only in the mind – this is, after all, the basis of the distinction between primary and secondary qualities. However, Berkeley asks, is it possible to conceive of primary qualities independently of the secondary ones? Can you imagine a thing with a shape, perhaps moving, but without a colour? Berkeley argues that you cannot. If you cannot conceive of primary qualities existing independently of the secondary ones, and if you admit that the secondary qualities are themselves mind-dependent, then the primary ones have to be mind-dependent too. If it turns out that what you thought was mind-independent is inconceivable without something that is itself mind-dependent, then the allegedly mind-independent thing is mind-dependent after all. Put simply, Berkeley is arguing that Locke's distinction collapses: both primary and secondary qualities can exist only in the mind.

You can change tack and argue that there is a particularly glaring problem with Berkeley's view, a difficulty which has something to do with the explanation of perceptual events themselves. Suppose it is Christmas, and you hang the stockings by the chimney with care. You buy your mother those golf balls she has been coveting, and you place them, one by one, into a stocking. You stand back and admire your handiwork, but then recall Berkeley's claim that objects are nothing but collections of sensory ideas which can exist only in the mind of a perceiver. No one currently perceives your mother's golf balls, as they are hidden away in the stocking. Slightly panicked, you rush over and empty the stocking on the floor, and the golf balls roll out. Is Berkeley committed to the absurdity that the golf balls, while unperceived, winked out of existence? And if they did, what explains their sudden reappearance when you tipped out the stocking?

A materialist – someone who believes that not only minds and ideas but also mind-independent material objects exist – has an obvious explanation for this sort of perceptual event. The golf balls were always there, existing unperceived in the material world, ready to be seen again when the stocking is emptied. But Berkeley does not have recourse to matter. His universe is populated only with minds and the ideas in them. How, then, can he explain the persistence of objects, the regular, seamless nature of the experienced world?

A God of the gaps?

If ideas, including those golf balls, continue to exist when we take our eyes off them, Berkeley argues, then some other mind must have perceived them all the while. It is not just golf balls, but the entire universe which hums along when we blink or go to sleep or otherwise neglect it. Only an infinite mind is capable of all this, so Berkeley argues that the mind of God keeps everything in existence, keeps perceiving the world, while our finite minds glimpse only a part of it.

Many blanch at Berkeley's solution to this problem. They claim that Berkeley is just positing a 'God of the gaps', wheeling in God to save a wobbly philosophical thesis. But for Berkeley it is quite the reverse. God is not shoring up a bogus metaphysics; the existence of God is proven by the metaphysical view. Berkeley has arguments for the claim that the very notion of material substance is incoherent or otherwise suspect. He also agrees with his detractors that some explanation of the regularity of perceptual events is required. If objects seem to carry on when we do not perceive them, and the explanation positing a material substratum is a non-starter, then there must be some other mind responsible for the persistence of objects.

The mind in question cannot be finite, and it also seems to be benevolent. Appearances exhibit a regularity which we can come to know and exploit, which can help us live our lives comfortably. The golf balls stay where we left them. For Berkeley 'every thing we see, hear, feel or in any wise perceive by sense, [is] a sign or effect of the power of God'. Berkeley is not using God to save him from an embarrassing objection. Instead a proof of the existence of God is for him in every aspect of the universe, in every one of our perceptions. By cropping matter from the picture, Berkeley puts God at the very centre of everything. So much for the godless materialism of Hobbes, Locke and, in general, the empirical view of the world.

It is not clear, though, that Berkeley's move works. First of all, Berkeley is arguing from the existence of some large, benevolent mental activity to the conclusion that the mentality in question is God as traditionally conceived. At least a premise or two are owed here. Second, and probably worse, Berkeley is replacing one suspect thing, material substance, with another, God. Even if we admit that the notion of matter is somehow confused or mysterious, replacing a material mystery with a divine one is no advance.

It is also not clear that Berkeley's general aim of restoring the common-sense view is a success. He claims:

> That the things I see with my eyes and touch with my hands exist, really exist, I make not the least question. The only thing whose existence we deny is that which *philosophers* call Matter or corporal substance. And in doing of this there is no damage done to the rest of mankind, who, I daresay, will never miss it.

Is it not a piece of common sense that the things we touch with our hands are made up of something more than our ideas? Isn't the denial of mind-independent objects a kind of scepticism, not an expression of common sense?

The questions can linger, along with the worry that Berkeley has offered us a series of arguments which are, at the very same time, irrefutable but unpersuasive. As Hume says of Berkeley, his arguments are unanswerable, but we still refuse to accept his conclusions. How could this be? Perhaps we are treading among beliefs we simply cannot be talked out of, particularly the view that there is more to the world than minds and perceptions. Insouciance, though, is no argument; it is no better than kicking a stone. We will have to do more than this if we want a proper answer to Berkeley.

In his lifetime, David Hume was called 'Le Bon David' in French salons, 'Saint David' in Scotland, and 'The Terrible David' by his theistic detractors. Thinkers since his death have given us a ready supply of other characterizations. He has been called the greatest Scottish philosopher ever, and there is little doubt that he deserves this praise. In some quarters, he is considered the greatest philosopher of the eighteenth century. Do bear in mind, as you think about this, that the eighteenth century is not exactly populated by philosophical slouches – it had Berkeley, Voltaire, Rousseau, Kant, Bentham, Reid and Fichte in it. Many regard Hume as the greatest empiricist, or at least the most uncompromising empiricist. Some view him as the greatest philosopher in the sceptical tradition, perhaps the oldest and worthiest tradition of all.

However you choose to characterize him, Hume is a philosophical giant, although he was not recognized as such until after his death. He published the monumental *Treatise of Human Nature* in 1739; the book offers a fresh and comprehensive analysis of the understanding, the passions and morality, but few read it. Of those who managed to find a way through it, not many understood it. It has been said that Reid and Kant were Hume's only contemporaries with the capacity to understand him, and both cite him as the catalyst for their best works. But, as Hume put it, the book 'fell dead-born from the press without reaching such distinction as even to excite a murmur among the zealots'.

He reworked the book, producing two polished, shorter, more digestible portions of its central thoughts: *An Enquiry Concerning Human Understanding* and *An Enquiry Concerning the Principles of Morals*. It would be a mistake to think of the shorter works as just popularized versions of the larger *Treatise*. Hume's bold aim in the original work was to found a 'science of human nature', just as Newton formulated a science of motion. Hume initially hoped that he might uncover rock-bottom principles or rules which underpin human understanding, emotion, rationality, and so on. This hope, and the attending apparatus of rules and laws of the mind, is down-played or absent in the later enquiries. Whole topics are missing from the shorter works – notably Hume's famous treatment of the self – and it might be argued that the methods proper to the works are different too.

Our focus here is Hume's first *Enquiry*, on the nature of human understanding. It would be hard to argue that this is Hume's most important or best work – all of his philosophical writings stand together in importance, influence and philosophical brilliance. It is, however, probably the most representative of Hume's settled views. As he writes in an advertisement for the *Enquiry*: '. . . the Author desires, that the following Pieces may alone be regarded as contain-ing his philosophical sentiments and principles.' Calling the *Enquiry* a series of 'pieces' has seemed apt to many. The work is divided into 12 books, and on a first reading it is easy to see them as only partially connected. The topics do range widely, but the general position which emerges renders the whole coherent enough.

If the *Enquiry* has a stated aim, it is found in its first few pages, where Hume considers various species of philosophy. You can hear more than a little Locke in Hume's words; not enough to convince you that Hume is Locke's apostle, but enough to situate him in the empiricist tradition. You might recall that the aim of Locke's essay is to see what subjects the human mind really is able to think about pro-ductively, and he concludes that intuitive knowledge of self, demon-strative knowledge of God, and sensitive knowledge of external objects are all possible. Hume begins with much the same aim, and similar methods, but his conclusions about the scope of human understanding are clearly sceptical in nature. It turns out, for Hume, that our apparently unshakeable beliefs about the self and the world have no grounding at all in reason. (If you are curious about Hume's take on God, have a look at his *Dialogues Concerning Natural Religion*, a spectacular attack on arguments for God's existence. The book was considered so scandalous that it was only published posthumously, and the publisher refused to put its name on the book.)

Impressions and ideas

Hume begins, as does Locke, with a consideration of the contents of the mind, the objects of human understanding or – in Hume's terms – the perceptions of the mind or materials of thinking. These he divides into two: impressions and ideas. There is a clear distinction, already noticed by Locke, between actually feeling pain, heat, warmth, anger, seeing a landscape, hearing a siren or desiring a cool drink, and later recalling or imagining these experiences. Hume uses the term 'impressions' to pick out 'all our more lively perceptions, when we hear, or see, or feel, or love, or hate, or desire, or will'. Ideas are the less forcible, faint copies of these, called up by memory or the imagination.

What, for Hume, is the relationship between ideas and impressions? He claims that 'all our ideas or more feeble perceptions are copies of our impressions or more lively ones'. Ideas, in other words, are derived solely from experience. Of course, Hume knows that some ideas – say, my idea of a unicorn – do not correspond exactly to a particular impression. But the component parts of my idea of a unicorn – ideas of horses and horns – are copies of things I have seen in the world. I have just combined ideas derived from experience in a novel way. The point is, for Hume, that although the mind might seem nearly unlimited in its capacity to imagine and wonder, the raw materials for its operations are always mined from impressions.

This is the kernel of empiricism, and Hume offers a few arguments for it. He suggests that you think about your own store of ideas and try to point to one which is not dependent on some original impression. Hume also goes straight for the rationalists' favourite innate idea – the idea of God – and shows that we can actually acquire it by thinking about the qualities of our own minds and then augmenting the good and the wise aspects without limit. Finally, he considers individuals who lack some sensory faculty or other – the blind, say – and notes that they have no ideas of colour. The explanation, he argues, is that ideas are copies of impressions, and if you have never had the relevant impressions, you stand no chance of having the corresponding ideas.

There are certain facts about impressions and ideas, and in Hume's hands these facts have far-reaching philosophical consequences. Compared to impressions, ideas are naturally faint and obscure, and it is easy to make two sorts of mistakes when thinking about them. First, you might mistake one idea for another, might think a conclusion about one is warranted when it turns out you are actually thinking about a different idea which only resembles it. Second, and worse, we use words to stand for ideas, and our speech can roll along happily even though it turns out that there is no fixed or determined idea corresponding to the relevant bits of our language. In a philosophical dispute, when we are not talking about horses and horns but very complex and abstract ideas, we can talk right past each other, mean different things by the very same words. We might even be arguing about nothing at all. Our dispute might be about illusory ideas, mere phantasms which have no grounding in experience – the philosophical equivalent of unicorns.

These reflections issue in a procedure for weeding out bogus ideas, finding a way through philosophical disputes, maybe even ending them. Hume writes:

> When we entertain, therefore, any suspicion, that a philosophical term is employed without any meaning or idea (as is but too frequent), we need but enquire, *from what impression is that supposed idea derived?* And if it be impossible to assign any, this will serve to confirm our suspicion. By bringing ideas into so clear a light, we may reasonably hope to remove all dispute, which may arise, concerning their nature and reality.

The fallout from these lines is staggering.

Consider the idea of an enduring self, a substantial something which persists throughout the many changes involved in living a life. I take it, for example, that I am essentially the same me this morning that I was when I went to bed last night. Not only this, but I think I am the same me I was right back to my misspent youth. I think I will be the same me for however long I am alive. No doubt some things have changed: I have grown taller, picked up a few scars, my hair seems to be a bit greyer. However, there seems to be something essential, the real me, which persists throughout all these accidental changes.

If you are persuaded by Hume's principle about the connection between ideas and impressions, and if you are convinced that his method for weeding out bogus ideas is the right one, then you have only to ask: From what impression is my idea of self derived? On looking inwards, Hume argues, he finds nothing but a series of fleeting impressions – hatred, love, heat, pain, sights, sounds, smells and the like – but nothing permanent, nothing which persists throughout the changes. No impression, in short, corresponds to our idea of self. It can join 'unicorn'; 'self' is a word for an illusory idea, a fiction of the imagination.

It gets much worse. Hume's take on the nature of human understanding begins with a distinction between two sorts of 'objects of human reason': relations of ideas and matters of fact. Relations of ideas are discoverable by the operation of reason alone. You can know that bachelors are unmarried males or that two times five is half of twenty by just thinking about the relations between the ideas in question. Matters of fact, though, are discoverable only via experience. Even if you meditate as much as you like on the proposition that the sun is shining, you will not know whether it is true unless you look out of the window. There is another difference between these two sorts of proposition. The contrary of a matter of fact is possible, but if you negate a true statement about the relation between ideas, you are left with a contradiction. The sun might not be shining, but there is no truth anywhere near the claim that bachelors are not unmarried males.

The problem of induction

With this distinction in hand, Hume focuses on what he takes to be the fundamental operation of the understanding. How, he asks, do we go beyond the present testimony of the senses or memory? How do we think our way from our current experiences to facts about things we are not currently experiencing – facts about the future or the past or just facts about present states of affairs beyond the narrow band of our current sensory horizon? I know that my cat Steve found his way into the living room last night because I can see tell-tale claw marks on the couch. The present testimony of my senses (the visual image of the claw marks) leads me to some past event (Steve menacing the couch) which I cannot now see. What underpins this sort of thinking?

Hume argues that all reasoning from present matters of fact to facts beyond them depends on causality. We take some aspect of our current sensory experience as a cause or effect of something we do not presently experience. I take the claw marks I can see as the effects of a prior cause, Steve sharpening his claws on the couch. How do we come to know about cause and effect? Hume argues that our knowledge cannot depend on the relations of ideas but must be derived entirely from experience. You might be an ace rationalist, a thinker second to none, but if you were presented with some gunpowder and had no relevant experiences, you could never know a thing about its effects. Just an inspection of gunpowder's sensible properties, in other words, is not enough to tell you that it explodes when touched with flame. That is something you can only come to know through experience (preferably at a safe distance).

And not just one or a few experiences, but many experiences are required. Over time, having observed enough gunpowder, you begin to anticipate the effects when you see the causes. Our knowledge of causation, the standard effects objects have on one another, comes only through considerable experience of the world. You know the billiard ball is going to move in such and such a direction when you strike it at a certain angle with the cue, but that is because you have spent a lot of time in pubs.

Well, what is the foundation of our conclusions from experience? Hume has argued that a number of experiences of causal conjunctions lead us to expect that those causal conjunctions will continue to hold in the future. We see many matches being struck (causes) which are then followed by the production of flame (effects). Why think, on examining the next match, that striking it will result in a flame? How does experience underpin our causal reasoning, our anticipation of effects when presented with causes? Hume's answer is induction.

All of our conclusions from experience, he argues, depend on the principle of induction: the future will be like the past. We have seen a number of matches being struck, and when we see the next one struck, we expect it to behave as the past ones have behaved. We have this expectation because we are thinking inductively. An inductive inference moves from a number of particular truths (striking this match resulted in flame, striking that match resulted in flame, and so on) to some general conclusion (striking any match produces a flame). What gets us from the particular truths to the general conclusion is the belief that the future will be like the past: in this case that future matches will behave like past matches have behaved.

Hume asks a final question: What proof do we have that the future will be like the past? What justifies our belief in the principle of induction? Either it is a relation of ideas, in which case we can see its truth by reflection, or it is a matter of fact, in which case we can come to know it through experience. This is Hume's Fork, and he argues that neither prong can serve up the justification we seek.

The claim that the future will be like the past cannot be a relation of ideas, because its negation implies no contradiction. The proposition that the future will not be like the past is entirely thinkable – there is no self-contradiction in imagining that the causal laws we think we have found will change in the future. There is no contradiction in thinking that striking a match will not result in a flame.

The claim that the future will be like the past cannot be grounded in matters of fact either. This would amount to the claim that the future will be like the past because, in the past, the future was like the past. It is arguing in a circle, using the principle of induction to ground the principle itself, and a circular argument is no justification.

It is worth pausing over this series of reflections for a moment.

Hume argues that our justification for going beyond the present testimony of our senses and memory is causal reasoning. Thinking about causes itself depends on having a fair bit of experience and using induction to come to conclusions about causes and effects. Induction depends on the principle of induction, and this principle, Hume argues, has no justification in reason – it cannot be grounded in either reflection or sensation. What justifies inductive thinking, if not reason? Hume's answer is custom or habit. When we are presented with a match, long experience puts us in the habit of expecting fire. There is no rational justification for this expectation; it is just a feature of human nature. We cannot help it.

That might not be enough for you: you might have hoped that there is something more to the justification of our beliefs about the world than simply a habit of mind. Hume's claim is that beyond some maths, a clutch of definitions, and our current experiences, knowledge has no rational justification at all. It is not clear that this is enough for Hume either. Philosophy leads him to scepticism, he says, but human nature seems to provide him with a kind of solution to sceptical doubts – if not a solution, then a distraction. Ensconced in his study, scepticism holds sway, but the moment he steps outside and 'makes merry with his friends', the dark conclusions fade, even seem a little ridiculous to him. Human nature, if not rational at bottom, seems to nudge us away from worrying too much about our irrationality. It is a consolation, perhaps, but not much of one.

9   The Social Contract
Jean-Jacques Rousseau (1712–78)

Jean-Jacques Rousseau's philosophy, like his life, is a little rough around the edges. Both contain tensions, even outright contradictions, and it might be these which make both so interesting. You can find an uplifting rags-to-riches story in his life, particularly if you look away from its dispiriting end. You can also see him as a debauched Lothario, even a moral monster, particularly if you pay attention to the fact that he dispatched his five children to an orphanage shortly after each one was born. His philosophy mirrors his life: it is certainly as passionate. It has flaws and difficulties in it too, and probably all of this makes it possible to read so much into his work. His books were burned in his lifetime, and warrants were issued for his arrest because of them, but his body is now reverently interred in the Pantheon. His thoughts have been taken up by populist totalitarians and libertarians in almost equal measure. Successive generations, with radically varying agendas, all find something true in Rousseau. The rough-edged and mercurial nature of his philosophy makes this possible.

His best work, no doubt, is *The Social Contract.* It is not easy to understand the value of the book without recognizing the extraordinary departure it makes from earlier versions of social contract theory. So Hobbes and Locke will be with us most of the way. We will also consider some of the rough edges in Rousseau's political philosophy.

Hobbes, you might recall, was the first to attempt to ground the nature of political obligation in reason, rather than myth or the divine right of the ruler. Rousseau certainly is in this rational tradition, although he blends it with the occasional appeal to the heart and a measure of sentimentality. Insofar as the conjunction is possible, he is a rational romantic. Like Hobbes, he maintains that talk of a social contract is what confers legitimacy to the state, but he departs from Hobbes very quickly. This departure begins with his quite different conception of human nature.

Human nature

Hobbes outlines a number of psychological factors which lead ungoverned human beings inexorably to a state of war against each other. Fear, competition and a desire for glory – as well as the simple physical fact that humans are by nature equally vulnerable to harm – result in an unsavoury picture of the natural human and his short life in Hobbes' thinking. It is this image which reinforces the rational motivation underpinning the social contract: getting out of the state of nature is the prudent thing to do. Staying out of it is what justifies Hobbes' claim that the monarch's power must be absolute. Rousseau's conception of human nature is nowhere near as pessimistic – it might even be inspiring, if you have the right sort of disposition – so it is only to be expected that both the social contract itself and the kind of government power it justifies are by his lights very different.

People are naturally good, on Rousseau's view, and in a sense it is society which corrupts them. A little care is needed here, as it is easy to misinterpret Rousseau's point. In earlier essays, Rousseau really does seem to have it in for civilization. All the sciences, he says elsewhere, have dubious origins: astronomy is rooted in the superstitions of astrology, mathematics is born of greed, and even physics comes from vain curiosity. Metallurgy and farming were a mistake. Ungoverned humans are innocent, free, even noble, but the state brings with it corruption, inequality and servitude. He calms down a little in *The Social Contract* and the rhetorical flourishes are fractionally diminished, but he retains the view that natural human beings, people in the state of nature, are not exactly Hobbesian brutes. He also continues with the claim that civilization can be a corrupting influence, but his mature view can only be understood with a number of provisos.

Many jump the gun, though, and assume that Rousseau is advocating a return to the state of nature, calling for us to throw off the vile trappings of society. One unscrupulous gardener I have known refused to mow the lawn, claiming that he was persuaded of

Rousseau's principles. This is nowhere near Rousseau's point. Society can corrupt, but it need not do so. In fact, Rousseau argues that it is only through civilized interactions that the natural man can become something more, something better. He can trade up from a life of amoral self-preservation to a moral life, a better kind of freedom. Rather than merely possessing things by force, he can have legal entitlements. What is more, he gains moral freedom, the freedom to choose rather than be bound by blind appetite. Instead of 'stupid, limited animal', society can enable the individual to become 'a creature of intelligence and a man'. This is not the language expected of a person who holds to the simple-minded conception of society as corrupting.

Nevertheless, Rousseau's language is sometimes unhelpful, can sometimes nudge the reader towards the conclusion that Rousseau is making the old and uncomplicated claim that civilization corrupts. 'Man is born free', he bristles, 'and everywhere he is in chains.' The point is that freedom is something we have from the start, but it is something we seem to have given up. It need not be this way. You can see a glimmer of this hope in Rousseau's statement of his aims in writing *The Social Contract*: 'My purpose is to consider if, in political society, there can be any legitimate and sure principle of government, taking men as they are, and laws as they might be'. Unlike Hobbes and Locke, Rousseau is engaged in hypothetical philosophy. He is not trying to say what it is which renders legitimate the state we have, but what a legitimate state might be like. Given a certain conception of human nature (men as they are), what should a state be like (laws as they might be)? It is the hypothetical status of the enquiry which makes Rousseau's thinking so attractive to people with revolution in mind.

What conception of human nature is operative in Rousseau's thinking? We have noticed that he thinks humans are naturally good, but it is probably best to understand Rousseau as meaning that people are potentially good. Strictly speaking, humans in Rousseau's state of nature are amoral, governed not by laws and moral principles but by appetite, instinct and, above all, the pre-reflective dictates of self-preservation. There is a kind of inbuilt freedom associated with all of this. The natural human looks after himself and is, therefore, his own master.

In his early writings, Rousseau argues that it is the advent of private property which brings about the downfall of the noble savage. 'The first man who, after fencing off a piece of land, took it upon himself to say "this is mine", and found people simple enough to believe him, was the real founder of civil society.' Once private property is on the cards, once it is possible to think of something as mine and not yours, inequality is born and the natural freedom of humanity dies. Those with more stuff become the masters of those with less.

The Social Contract

In *The Social Contract*, however, Rousseau sees a way out of all of this in a new conception of political obligation and state legitimacy – in 'laws as they might be'. In his largest departure from previous social contract theorists, Rousseau argues that it is possible for human beings to be both ruled and free. The problem, for Rousseau, is to find a form of government which 'will defend and protect with the whole common force the person and goods of each associate, and in which each, while uniting himself with all, may still obey himself alone and remain as free as before'. Rousseau, in other words, wants it both ways. He wants to ensure the sort of protection only a government can confer, along with the moral and civil virtues which attend it, while preserving and enhancing the freedom of the natural human. Hobbes and Locke both think that this is impossible: to get a government, they argue, you have to give up freedom.

Hobbes argues that people contract together to confer their liberty wholesale on the sovereign. Locke argues instead that people contract with the sovereign, giving up the lion's share of liberty, designating a disinterested judge or judges to defend their natural rights. For Rousseau, people can be both ruled and free if they rule themselves, and this is accomplished by keeping freedom in the hands of the people, who contract together to become jointly sovereign. The sovereign is no king or parliament, but the people considered as a whole.

The social contract, Rousseau argues, consists in the 'total alienation' of all rights by every member of the community to the community itself. This means that there is no one in particular – no king or small group of rulers – who gains some advantage in the bargain. Everyone loses just the same things, and everyone gains just the same things. Instead of an all-powerful monarch, the social contract creates 'a corporate body', composed of as many people as there are in the community.

It is important to keep an eye on Rousseau's terms in this connection. He says that the people who contract together are 'citizens' insofar as they have a share in the governmental power of the corporate body and 'subjects' insofar as they place themselves under its laws. You can begin to see that Rousseau's desire to preserve freedom and keep the rule of law imposes a kind of duality on him. He needs to think of people in two ways, as citizens and subjects, and you can wonder whether or not this is sustainable. If every contractor has an equal share in power, insofar as each is a citizen, then are we not more or less back in the state of nature, with each person considering just her own interests in making law? Part of Rousseau's solution to this problem consists in the denial that individuals who contract together retain rights. In lawmaking, individuals have no rights to claim, and therefore can consider only the common good in deciding what to do. The other part of Rousseau's answer has to do with the nature of the sovereign and the common good itself.

The sovereign and the general will

Rousseau says that the body politic created by the contract is 'the state' when passive and 'the sovereign' when active. It is important to note that his use of the word 'sovereign' is more than a little idiosyncratic, and it is not entirely clear what he means by it. He certainly does not mean the king or parliament or even what we mean when we talk about 'the administration'. In fact, Rousseau argues that the people as a whole should engage in legislation, that is to say that the people ought to get together to devise a system of law spelling out sanctions and rewards for certain actions. This activity is distinct from administration – actually passing judgement on individuals – which is something that the sovereign cannot do. Instead, the people grant a kind of contractual, temporary power to the administration to carry out its functions. The sovereign, it is clear, is not in the day-to-day business of government, at least not administrative government.

Rousseau makes a number of claims about the sovereign. He argues that it simply cannot have any interest contrary to the people's interests. It cannot be ill-intentioned, cannot have any motives other than the common good. Nor can it be wrong about what is in the common interest, unless it is somehow misinformed. Further, it is perpetually in the hands of the people: it cannot be handed over to a king or the administration. 'The Sovereign, merely by virtue of what it is, is always what it should be.'

Well, what could it possibly be? Take the claim that the sovereign cannot have any interest contrary to the people's interests. People obviously have very many interests, often competing or conflicting interests. So how could the sovereign fail to have interests contrary to the interests of at least some individuals? Insofar as an individual is a subject, his interests might conflict with those of the sovereign, but insofar as an individual is a citizen, his interests and the interests of the sovereign are the same. This is so, Rousseau argues, because the sovereign is an expression of the general will.

The general will arises, somehow, through group decision-making. In the shift from the state of nature to civilized life, human beings are forced to consider more than their own interests. Recall that the social contract not only makes government possible, but, for Rousseau, it also involves humanity in a kind of transformation from brutes to moral, thinking, civic-minded human beings. Part of the transformation consists in a shift from the self-interested demands of survival to the recognition that the interests of others demand attention, even the possibility that the interests of others should come before one's own interests at least some of the time. A body politic is more than just a collection of self-interested people. For Rousseau, it is an organism, and the organism has a general will.

Some make sport of all of this and find more than enough rough edges to get some objections going. Could the claim actually be that a new entity is brought into the world, literally an organism, when all contract together? Some wonder, uncharitably, what this creature is up to or where it is spends the night. Working out what the thing wills, it is claimed, is beyond us. Others claim, a little more charitably, that talk of an organism is just a literary device. Rousseau's point is that something like a will can be discerned in the operations of a body politic. After all, collections of people can seem to have a will – we talk of things like 'the discontent of the working classes'. We make sense of this talk without being literalists, so why not take it that Rousseau is talking about something similar with regard to a whole community?

The truth is probably somewhere in between a literal and literary interpretation of Rousseau. Although some go down this route, it is not clear that the general will is the sum of individual wills with the conflicts of interest factored out. Others take it that the general will is just the will of the majority. But both of these interpretations fail to take account of Rousseau's distinction between the will of all and the general will. He says that the will of all is just what everyone, in fact, happens to will, but in a sense the general will is what everyone ought to will. It is the will of citizens thinking like citizens, concerned to do their civic duty and look out for one another. It is an ideal, and maybe this explains the bold claims noticed earlier: that the sovereign cannot have any interest contrary to the people's interests, cannot be ill-intentioned, and cannot have any motives other than the common good. If the sovereign is an expression of the general will – and the general will is a kind of ideal, the purified will of the citizens actuated only by their common interests as a people – then maybe these claims make a kind of sense.

Forced to be free

This line of thinking also sheds a little light on a particularly troubling claim made in *The Social Contract*. Rousseau argues that whoever refuses to obey the general will must be forced to obey it, must be 'forced to be free'. If the general will is a normative conception, an ideal which tells us how things ought to be, then someone who refuses to go along with it is outside morality, still stuck with other beasts in the state of nature. Freedom consists in part in acting morally, for the welfare of others, rather than being bound by instinct. Someone who does not go along with the general will fails to exercise the freedom of moral choice, is just a slave to the passions. There is more than a rough edge here, and some have noted, perhaps uncharitably, that freedom might consist for Rousseau in the freedom to do what the police tell you to do.

There is something more troubling in all of this, namely the possibility that there just is no unified general will, however you try to understand it. People can have competing interests, even rational competing interests, even perfectly civic-minded, rational competing interests. If this is so, how could there be just one general will? How you choose to smooth out this and the other rough edges will lead you to different conclusions about the value, and the point, of Rousseau's thinking.

10   Critique of Pure Reason
Immanuel Kant (1724–1804)

In a letter to Moses Mendelssohn, Kant says this about the *Critique of Pure Reason*: 'although the book is the product of twelve years of reflection, I completed it hastily, in perhaps four or five months, with the greatest attentiveness to its content but less care about its style and ease of comprehension'. Indeed.

Although it is certainly astonishing to think that the book took Kant only a few months to write, there is nothing at all surprising in his admission that style and ease of comprehension were not foremost in his mind during the writing itself. The book is a labyrinth: its arcane structure induces something akin to conceptual vertigo; sentences and paragraphs of awe-inspiring length slouch past mercilessly; new and highly technical vocabulary is introduced and then employed with panic-inducing irregularity. What is more, Kant's topic is no walk in the park. He is attempting to formulate nothing less than the solution to all metaphysical problems, and his answer requires a comprehensive and earth-shattering revolution in epistemology. You can furrow a philosopher's brow from a distance just by mentioning the *Critique of Pure Reason*.

Despite all of this, there is simply no question that Kant's book is one of the greatest works of philosophy ever written. We will first consider the problem Kant tries to solve in the book and then have a look at his solution. You might find all of this difficult. Console yourself with the fact that if you do find it difficult, you are probably seeing it for what it is. Kant is not easy.

The trouble with metaphysics

Kant begins by noting that metaphysics has not enjoyed the successes of other disciplines such as mathematics and the natural sciences. Metaphysics seems to flounder in contradiction and controversy. For example, equally compelling arguments are offered for and against the claim that the world has a beginning in time and is spatially limited, that every composite substance consists of simple substances, that free will exists, and that there is a God. These topics are the bread and butter of metaphysics, but we seem left with either equally weighted dogmatic assertions for the truth or falsity of such claims or, perhaps worse, the possibility of the truth of scepticism.

The failure of metaphysics as compared to the many discoveries of mathematics and the natural sciences is particularly troubling for Kant, and it is not difficult to see why. Two philosophical schools were at the forefront of philosophy in Kant's day: rationalism and empiricism. Rationalists hold that at least some metaphysical truths are known independently of sense experience. Descartes, you might recall, thought that the existence of God could be proven by reflection on the concept of God as a being with no defects. Empiricists hold that the contents of the mind are stocked entirely by sense experience, and if any metaphysical truths are known, they must somehow be secured through the manipulation of ideas rooted in sensation. You can think of the discoveries of mathematics as examples of the successful use of rationalist tools and the discoveries of the natural sciences as examples of the successful use of empiricist tools. Why have both schools failed so comprehensively in metaphysics when success elsewhere seems to prove the value of their presuppositions and methods, disparate though they might be?

The trouble, for Kant, is that reason seems to be up to the job in some areas but not others. Reason gets underway and makes progress in mathematics and enquires into the nature of the natural world, but when reason turns to metaphysical problems, it goes belly-up. What is alarming is that we cannot seem to help it. Reason is drawn to metaphysics; metaphysical questions seem to demand answers. But our best attempts at dealing with metaphysics – rationalism and empiricism – are both failures.

Kant thinks both empiricism and rationalism are wrong. What is needed, he argues, is something entirely new: a new way of thinking about the role of reason in particular and the mind in general which explains both the failures and the successes of reason. We arrive at the new view, he claims, by embarking on a critique or self-examination of reason, in the hope of delineating the proper employment of reason itself. Kant, in almost stirring language, calls upon 'reason to undertake anew the most difficult of all its tasks, namely, that of self-knowledge, and to institute a tribunal which will assure to reason its lawful claims, and dismiss all groundless pretensions, not by despotic decrees, but in accordance with its own eternal and unalterable laws.' This is to undertake a critique of pure reason.

Kant's problem

You can think of the problem which exercises Kant in a number of ways. He is certainly trying to resolve the disputes of metaphysics. One party to the dispute, scepticism ('the euthanasia of pure reason'), is particularly worrying for him, and many see Kant as formulating a reply to scepticism, an answer to Hume's philosophy in particular. But he is up to much more than just the refutation of scepticism. Kant himself maintains that he is trying to show how metaphysics is possible. Metaphysics, as Kant understands it, is reason's attempt to think beyond the boundaries of sensation. If you want to get to the nut of the problem and understand it in Kant's terms, I am afraid that you will have to consider two difficult distinctions: the analytic/synthetic distinction and the *a priori/a posteriori* distinction.

To use Kant's language, some knowledge claims are analytic, and by this he means that some sentences ascribe a property to a concept, and the property itself is already contained in the concept. For example, if you know what a triangle is, you will see the truth of the analytic statement, 'Triangles have three sides.' You will see this truth by analysing the concept of a triangle and finding three-sidedness in it. You need not look around for a triangle to know that the sentence is true. Other truths, though, are synthetic, and by this Kant means that some sentences ascribe more to a concept than is contained within it, synthesize different concepts into an informative truth. For example, you might hear that 'Mel has a triangle tattooed to his arm'. The concept of Mel, whatever it might contain, does not contain the necessity of having a triangle tattooed to his arm. If the sentence is true, analysis alone will not deliver its truth – you will have to ask Mel to roll up his sleeve.

Kant claims that analytic truths are known *a priori* ('prior to experience'), and synthetic truths are known *a posteriori* ('after experience'). *A priori* truths are necessarily true; negate one and you are left with a contradiction. *A posteriori* truths are merely contingent; they depend on how the world actually is. You might already suspect that rationalists are in the *a priori*, analytic business and empiricists are occupied by *a posteriori*, synthetic truths. So far, so good.

However, if metaphysics is possible, Kant argues, there must be synthetic *a priori* truths, truths which are necessary and can be known independently of experience, but, at the same time, truths which claim more than could possibly be delivered by the mere analysis of the concepts in question. Metaphysics, in other words, seems to require strange, hybridized propositions. It requires truths known *a priori* which somehow go beyond what might be derived from the analysis of the components of concepts. Kant's question, then, is this: How are synthetic *a priori* truths possible? Asking this, for Kant, is asking how metaphysics is possible.

The Copernican revolution

The answer requires a complete reconsideration of the nature of the mind. Kant claims that solving the problems of metaphysics demands a revolution in thought of Copernican proportions. Just as the Copernican revolution turns everything on its head by showing that the sun, not the earth, is at the centre of the solar system, Kant's revolution in epistemology places the properties of the mind, not the properties of objects, at the centre of our understanding of the empirical world.

Both rationalists and empiricists, in their own ways, believe that an understanding of the natural world requires a match between whatever is going on in the perceiver's head and whatever is going on in the world. We come to know things by getting our minds to conform to the world. Suppose that there really is some whiskey in the jar out there in the world. Genuinely coming to know this might consist in having a corresponding mental image of the jar in your head or having a proposition – 'there's whiskey in the jar' – flitting through your mind. Both rationalists and empiricists talk about the natural world imprinting or stamping itself on the mind, like a signet ring impressing an image on a wax seal. The mind, on this view, is working properly when it passively mirrors nature.

Kant's revolution consists in the claim that the mind is active, not passive. The mind does not merely reflect the world; in a sense, the mind's activity constitutes the world. To know the world of experience, it is not the mind which must conform to the world, but the world which must conform to the mind. The mind actively shapes and categorizes experience, turns it into a world of objects in space and time, standing in causal relations and obeying other rules. The mind imposes structure, creates a world of experience we can come to know. Empiricists, rationalists and sceptics wonder how it is that our minds might match up to the world. For Kant, this is the wrong question. What we need to ask is: How do our minds constitute the world?

Kant maintains that space and time are 'forms of sensible intuition' – he uses the word 'form' to distinguish space and time from the contents of sensory experience, that is to say that he is talking about space and time themselves as opposed to the objects we experience in space and time. By this he means that spatial and temporal relations are part of the structuring activities of the mind. We experience a world of objects, located in space and changing over time, because space and time are subjective forms of sensation. You can come close to making sense of this by thinking of a person wearing rose-coloured glasses. Everything that person sees ends up with a reddish tint, because everything that person sees has to pass through the lenses. The world we sense is ordered in space and time, because space and time are the forms of our sensory experience – everything we experience has to pass through our spatial and temporal lenses.

Sensory intuitions are not enough for knowledge, Kant argues. Intuitions must be 'brought under concepts', which is to say that sensory experience is further shaped and ordered by additional mental operations, further categorized. Kant identifies 12 categories: unity, plurality, totality, reality, negation, limitation, substance, causality, reciprocity, possibility, actuality and necessity. Once intuitions are shaped by these fundamental categories, we come to have experience of the objective world.

Kant's argument for the existence of the categories, his proof that the world we experience really is shaped by them, is probably the most difficult part of the *Critique*. He calls it the 'Transcendental Deduction of the Categories'. We cannot arrive at the categories just by looking around because, if he is right, the categories are already built into whatever we experience. Instead, the deduction must transcend experience. Kant argues that the only way to prove the validity of the categories is to show that they are presupposed in any possible experience. The gist of the deduction is as follows. The kind of inner, subjective experience a subject has – the sort of thing even Descartes admits he cannot doubt – is possible only if there is an objective world. In other words, I can have an experience I actually do have only if there is an objective, empirical world of objects in space and time, standing in causal relation – only if, that is to say, the world out there conforms to the categories in the mind.

Reflection on the categories leads Kant to what he has been after all along: the synthetic, *a priori* propositions which make metaphysics possible. The concept of cause, for example, can only be applied on the assumption that every event has a cause. In other words, we can only have the experience we actually have if every event really does have a cause. The concept of substance can be applied only on the assumption that substance remains permanent throughout all change. In other words, we can only have the experience of change we actually have if substance underpins change. The same applies for all of the categories he identifies. The propositions themselves are *a priori* (you can tell because they are necessary) and synthetic (you can tell because the concept of, say, cause does not contain within it the concept of every event having a cause).

Speculative metaphysics

Before you get out the champagne, though, there is a very large proviso attached to this. Kant argues that the categories and the metaphysical principles derived from them apply only to the world of appearances. Kant makes a distinction between appearances and the things-in-themselves. The empirical world, the world of objects in space and time, is the world as we experience it, a world of appearances. But what that world is like in itself, apart from the categorizing activities of the mind, is something we can never know. Space and time, substance and cause, are empirically real, but no part of the world as it is in itself.

Kant is placing a curb on the proper employment of the categories of the mind, and as he does so he answers some of the questions posed at the start of the *Critique*. What explains the contradictions of metaphysics? The controversies arise as a result of reason trying to apply the categories it simply must use to make sense of the world of appearances to the world as it is in itself. It is reason going beyond its proper employment. So some metaphysical claims are preserved, but 'speculative' metaphysics – characterized by the hope of thinking of the world as it is in itself – is undermined.

Think about causation. The mind can only experience a world of objects in terms of the rule that every event has a cause. But if the mind tries to apply this perfectly good principle to the universe as a whole, tries to speculate about something which is not a possible object of experience, then we end up in contradiction. If we ask, 'Does the universe have a beginning in time?', then we are trying to regard the universe itself as a substance, an object of experience in causal relations. We are trying to apply categories which are properly applied only to particular appearances, but the universe is no such object. You can extend all of this by thinking for a moment about other metaphysical entities which are not objects of experience, such as God and the soul.

There is nothing wrong with reason as such – it has given us mathematics and the means to study the natural world. It can even, through self-examination, discover certain metaphysical truths. What it cannot do, though, is engage in speculative metaphysics. It cannot go beyond the bounds of sense, cannot apply its categories to the world as it is in itself.

You might think that Kant has closed speculative metaphysics off once and for all. Despite the provisos concerning the proper employment of reason, there is still room for talk of God, the soul and freedom in Kant – plenty of room. Kant argues that metaphysical excesses must be purged from our conception of the world of objects, but what of things as they are in themselves? He shows that human beings, for example, insofar as they are things which appear in the objective world, are as bound by causal relations as any other object. But what humans are in themselves is something we cannot know, at least not by thinking about ourselves as appearances. There is room for freedom, and in other works Kant formulates a remarkably powerful conception of morality based on it.

Kant's *Critique* is only a part of a much larger philosophical system. It is fair to say that almost all of it has been influential and has changed the face of philosophy. Certainly German philosophy in particular and Continental philosophy in general are what they are largely because of Kant. No doubt phenomenalists like Mill and eventually Russell felt Kant's influence too. Perhaps most surprisingly, given the rigidity of Kant's conception of the categories of the understanding, Kant's philosophy has given rise to a kind of relativism. If you buy into Kant's notion that the mind plays an active part in shaping the objective world but refuse to go along with the notion that the categories of the mind are the same for everyone, you end up with the view that people live in different worlds. This sort of thing probably would have appalled Kant. The thought can be a perversely consoling one, as you sweat your way through Kant's *Critique*.

11   The Phenomenology of Spirit
G. W. F. Hegel (1770–1831)

No one finds Hegel easy. Those who comment on Hegel, particularly since the start of the twentieth century, use the words 'impenetrable', 'difficult', 'incomprehensible', 'obscurantist' and, in less charitable moments, 'unspeakable'. Hegel's style is certainly part of the problem. He writes in such a way that you have to come to his work already knowing something about him in order to make sense of it. He is, in other words, not particularly smooth sailing for the novice student. There can seem to be no obvious way in. Instead you have to read and re-read more or less everything he writes, hoping eventually for a momentary flicker of understanding. Once this hits you, though, the clouds really do break a little.

His approach makes matters even worse. Hegel is not dealing with individual philosophical questions as we know them. He is a system builder, perhaps the last great system builder, and his writing offers nothing less than a conception of more or less everything.

You can find your way into Hegel, a little, by thinking about him as a reaction to Kant. Recall that Kant argues for a version of idealism, transcendental idealism, in which the mind actively structures the empirical world. According to Kant, the *a priori* forms of sensible intuition, space and time, as well as the categories of the understanding, ensure that whatever is given to us in sensory perception is structured and ordered into a world of objects. Thus, for Kant, the world we experience is what it is because of the activities of the mind. While Kant argues that the categories are written in stone – the categories are the same for any mind which experiences a world of objects as such – the philosophers who follow Kant largely reject his absolutism in favour of some species of relativism. For them different categories and, therefore, different worlds are possible.

Instead of thinking of individual minds as shaping reality, Hegel argues for absolute idealism. Here the view is that reality is not shaped by individual minds, but a single Cosmic Mind, which Hegel calls, 'Spirit'. You can think of this Mind as a thing trying to understand itself, as its categories or modes of understanding change with the times. This is not quite right, however, as for Hegel there is no genuine difference between reality and the Spirit which shapes or categorizes it. For Hegel, the whole of human history is Spirit coming to understand itself as reality. This, in a nutshell, is the key to understanding Hegel's thinking.

You can try coming at this tenet from other directions. A large part of Hegel's main claim is that the usual picture of the individual knower on the one hand and the particular object known on the other is a false one. Consciousness and the world itself are integrated. Consciousness is not really a discrete property of individuals, nor is the self something inside us. Instead, we are all parts of a single, whole, conscious Spirit, which is, itself, everything. This is not to say that the whole of reality is a unified substance; on Hegel's view, it is a complex system of Spirit, of which we are component parts.

If that did not help, you can try thinking again about Kant. As noted a moment ago, Kant argues that the categories are fixed, and there is just one reality for any subject which experiences a world of objects. Later German idealists – Fichte, for example – argue that there are different ways of 'seeing' the world; one might view the world objectively, scientifically or as a moral realm wherein one acts. Hegel argues that there are very many ways of viewing the world, numerous 'forms of consciousness'. But we cannot simply choose them; we cannot decide which form to take up. Instead, which view we have is fixed by our historical moment. Further, and this is probably Hegel's largest insight, the forms of consciousness evolve: better or perhaps more complete ones emerge as part of a large, historical process which tends towards a perfect view of the world. Throughout this historical process, Spirit comes to know itself better, truth develops and, in a literal sense, so does reality. History, in other words, is going somewhere, and Hegel studies it, teasing out its meaning. He is, in this sense, the first philosopher of history.

The dialectic

Hegel argues that the historical process is dialectical in nature. 'Dialectic' is an ancient Greek word for a certain sort of reasoning, exemplified in Plato's dialogues. The word was probably at first only associated with questions and answers, but in Hegel's hands it outlines a process of reasoning or logic. A particular claim is made (thesis), as its contradictions are drawn out and rendered explicit; a new conception is arrived at which emphasizes these contradictions (antithesis), and finally a resolution or blending of the two views is reached (synthesis). Hegel sees the whole of human history as exhibiting this sort of pattern, with a particular time holding to some conception of things, that conception containing within itself certain contradictions or difficulties which eventually become explicit, those contradictions being transcended by a new conception of things, and so on. Throughout it all, Spirit is coming to know itself better, until an ultimate state, Absolute Knowing, is realized.

The Phenomenology of Spirit is Hegel's attempt to sift through history with this dialectical process in mind. Marx, a student of Hegel who obviously took him very seriously, called the book 'the true birthplace and secret of Hegel's philosophy'. For Hegel, phenomenology is the study of appearances, phenomena, the way things seem to us insofar as we are perceivers, as opposed to metaphysics, the science of what truly is. 'Spirit' is Hegel's world for the Cosmic Mind which comes to know itself through the historical, dialectical process just scouted. So the title of the book suggests that here Hegel is examining the workings of Spirit as it appears to human beings. The book, by Hegel's lights, is nothing less than the truth about human history, what it all means and where we are headed.

In the Preface, Hegel says something about how the Absolute realizes itself, that is to say, comes to know itself. There are smaller dialectical moments, sub-dialectics working themselves out in parts of history, as well as a large historical trend which has three parts. First, consciousness is aware of just the sensible world; then consciousness becomes aware of itself. Hegel argues that in self-awareness consciousness negates or dominates the merely living and in so doing becomes a subject which experiences objects. Third, this false diversity is itself negated, and Spirit finally recognizes itself for what it is, that is to say, consciousness recognizes that both consciousness and the sensible world are one. If this does not yet make much sense, perhaps it will help to have a closer look at some of the processes the book describes. *The Phenomenology* falls into several parts, each examining a stage in or aspect of the historical process.

Consciousness and self-consciousness

Consider Section A, 'Consciousness'. Here, Hegel takes up three possible epistemological relations between consciousness and the objects which appear to it, and in each case he tries to show that one relation leads on to the next. The first and barest is sense-certainty, in which consciousness merely encounters an object perceptually but does not make much out of it: the thing is simply 'before the eyes'. The second, perception, involves consciousness distinguishing the properties of a thing without grasping the underlying nature of the thing itself. The third, understanding, is an attempt on the part of the knowing subject to come to terms with the underlying nature of objects, an attempt to get at the things behind the properties.

Hegel finds each sort of relation in the history of human beings' efforts to come to know the natural world. We begin by rooting knowledge just in sensation, which ultimately fails, because the moment we take sensations as the objects of knowledge, their immediacy is lost – they become something else. Our attempts to know based on perception reveal only that we know bundles of properties, with nothing but a mysterious 'substance' underlying them. An attempt to say what these properties are rooted in, a scientific understanding of things, leaves us with a long list of unknowable, alien forces. We end up with the view that trying to understand the world by pinning down sensation leaves us with no access to reality. What is needed, Hegel argues, is a consideration not only of consciousness, but also of self-consciousness.

In Part B, 'Self-Consciousness', Hegel considers our conception of ourselves as actors. The section contains probably the most famous example used to flesh out the nature of dialectical thinking, which Hegel calls 'the independence and dependence of self-consciousness: lordship and bondage'. We might think of animals as merely conscious, little appetite machines which are not self-reflective. Human beings, though, have more than just appetites. We have desires, and among those desires is the desire to be recognized as an independent self by others. Peering into history, we see feudal lords destroying their rivals in an effort to be recognized as powerful, free individuals. Some rivals are spared and become mere objects or slaves in the service not only of the lord's needs, but also in his desire to be seen as a powerful agent, a conqueror. However, in functioning as a servant, the slave attains a kind of value, realizes that he is, in fact, needed by the master. The drive for independent selfhood on the part of the lord results in a kind of servitude, a dependence on the slave. The thesis here is the drive towards independence; the antithesis is the master's eventual dependence on the servant.

The attempted synthesis is found in the struggle for free self-consciousness. When Spirit fails to find freedom through the interaction of two self-consciousnesses, it turns back in on itself in a novel way. Consciousness attempts to find freedom in itself, by renouncing a need for others. Hegel cites various attempts by later Roman thinkers to do so, in particular the resurgent Stoics and their steadfast indifference to the vagaries of existence, as evidence for an historical shift from dependence on others to a new kind of self-reliance. Finally, modern human beings look to reason, spirit and religion to achieve the necessary synthesis between consciousness and self-consciousness.

The rationality of the Enlightenment, as well as the rise of science, is characterized by Hegel as an effort to secure a kind of self-reliance or freedom through rational methods. These efforts, however, pull humanity too far in the direction of a cold and unsatisfying objectivity, and there follows a kind of resurgence of spirituality in the form of Romanticism, consciousness again looking inwards for resolution. Romantic thinking itself drags in a new moral thinking, in particular the view that the truth which is in an individual is felt by others, and thus others have an equal claim, are to be counted as valuable as oneself. It is in religion, finally, where humanity comes closest to the necessary and final synthesis. Hegel considers the whole history of religious thought, concluding that revealed faith, particularly Christianity, is the closest religion can get to absolute knowing, Spirit seeing itself for what it really is. Christ is God made flesh, on the Trinitarian view, and this is as near as phenomenology can come to the truth, namely that humanity is not distinct from ultimate reality, but a finite part of it.

So what Hegel is up to, generally, is rendering explicit a dialectic of ideas in human history – cashing out the rise and fall of religions, political and social relations, moralities and scientific theories. He sees none of them as entirely either true or false, but it is a mistake to conclude from this that Hegel was merely a relativist. There is truth and falsity in each historical moment, and each succeeding epoch gets closer to the final stage, absolute knowing, which Hegel sometimes thinks of as a kind of blurry, water-coloured utopia of human freedom and universal peace. What else could it be like, once everyone finally realizes that we are all really parts of one ultimate rationality? Before the realization, though, the road to the goal is more than a little unpleasant. If you want to think of Hegel himself as a product of his times, notice that he lived in the Napoleonic era, a time of bitter and costly wars. He calls the way to utopia 'the slaughter bench of history'.

The end

How close are we to the end? Part of Hegel's claim is that the goal of the process is nothing less than understanding the process itself, of seeing Spirit coming to know itself through history. Brace yourself. This is achieved by Hegel in the *Phenomenology*. If he is right, then the book itself is the culmination of the history of consciousness. You can rightly begin to smell a rat here. There is, in just about every age, the belief that the end is nigh, the hope or at least the thought that now is the moment of some great culmination. Can it all really have ended with the publication of the *Phenomenology*? Well, plainly it has not.

In fact, Hegelian thinking went on in earnest for more than a hundred years after the publication of the *Phenomenology*. As Marleau-Ponty puts it, 'All the great philosophical ideals of the past century, the philosophies of Marx, Nietzsche, existentialism and psycho-analysis had their beginning in Hegel'. Perhaps Marx is the most influential on this list of remarkable thinkers and movements. You can find a handle for thinking about Marx by regarding him as a kind of inversion of Hegel. Instead of thinking that ideas shape history, Marx argues that history or, anyway, historical facts, shape ideas. This might have been the largest thought, in terms of political fallout, of the past century or so, and its roots are certainly owed to Hegel. Hegelianism was probably the dominant philosophy, in both Europe and America, right up until the start of the twentieth century. You would be hard pressed to find even a handful of straightforward Hegelians alive today.

Hegelianism died because of a shift towards analysis in philosophy. Odd tenets were thought to follow from the view that reality is a single Cosmic Absolute. For example, the very idea of independently exist-ing things (wine bottles and corks) standing in relation to one another (the cork is in the wine bottle) is incoherent if Hegel is right. If reality itself is unified, then the appearance of distinct objects, as well as rela-tions between them, is illusory. Truths about particulars, on this view, can only be partial. G. E. Moore and those who followed him insisted on a return to the truths of common sense. The ordinary language movement attempted to return philosophical talk to its origins in everyday usage. Bertrand Russell's work on logic and mathematics made talk of concrete particular objects respectable and clear. A. J. Ayer and the Logical Positivists argued that the wild claims of Hegelian metaphysicians are literally nonsense. Against all of this, Hegel never stood a chance.

12   The World as Will and Representation
Arthur Schopenhauer (1788–1860)

Reflection on the lives of at least some philosophers can be dispiriting. When their books aren't being burnt, they are. The ones who
hold on to sanity for a while are variously arrested, poisoned, exiled
or forced to flee for their lives – a few have been shot, usually by their
students. When they mange to escape such fates, their lives are not
lived in celebration, and their deaths are frequently sad and lonely.
Even many of the great philosophers have been comprehensively
ridiculed in their lifetimes – others are just ignored until long after
their deaths. Rarely are philosophers carried out of the lecture hall on
the shoulders of their cheering and adoring students. Never do you
see their faces on the cover of *Vogue*.

Despite all of this, you can come around to the view that philosophers as a species seem fairly happy, certainly happier than you might
expect. They smile a lot. The autobiographies of at least some
philosophers brim with cheerfulness. Given the miserable lives of
philosophers, you would expect philosophy to contain some miserable books, some unhappy conclusions, but by and large it does not.
The legendary exception is Arthur Schopenhauer's *The World as Will
and Representation*. Schopenhauer's philosophy is spectacularly pessimistic, and so was Schopenhauer.

His mother tells us that from an early age he 'brooded on the
misery of things'. She operated a literary salon, and eventually threw
him out because her guests found his diatribes on the futility of existence a little tedious after a while. The broodings, though, produced a
book of genius. He wrote the first edition before he was 30, but no
one really noticed. He had to wait until he was 77 for interest in his
work to demand a third edition. What is remarkable is that throughout the intervening years he found no reason to make substantial
changes to the original manuscript. Instead, he added pages, spelling
out what he took to be the further consequences of truths already discovered and firmly established almost 50 years earlier.

He has some advice for you, if you want to get the most from the book. First, thoroughly familiarize yourself with Kant's philosophy. This might take you a while, because you must not only plough through all three of Kant's difficult *Critiques*, but Schopenhauer suggests that you also work through his own daunting treatment of Kant's categories of the understanding, *On the Fourfold Root of the Principle of Sufficient Reason*. Thus fortified, you must read *The World as Will and Representation* with great patience, no less than twice. If you think this advice is a little too demanding, he says that you should not bother reading the book at all. He suggests, instead, that you can still get your money's worth by using the book to fill a gap on the shelves of your library or maybe by leaving it on a table to impress the opposite sex. Or, he says, if you really do not want to read it, you might review it. This is probably Schopenhauer's best joke.

The book, Schopenhauer insists, imparts a single thought, though despite his best efforts he is unable 'to find a shorter way of imparting that thought than the whole of this book'. Here is a slightly shorter way: the world appears to us as representation, but its underlying nature is will. The work is divided into four books. The first deals with Schopenhauer's take on the world considered as appearance, idea or representation. The second, and perhaps most interesting, explains Schopenhauer's view that the entire world of appearance is nothing but objectified will. The third book contains Schopenhauer's treatment of aesthetics. The fourth is something of a solution to the horrors of existence in the denial of the will to live. We will consider some of this in what follows.

The Kantian background

Schopenhauer is quite right to say that some grounding in Kant is required for an understanding of his book, so this is where we will begin. Recall that Kant argues that the mind is active and that it is the *a priori* powers of the mind which have a role in shaping the nature of the experienced world. The forms of sensible intuition, space and time ensure that the objects we experience are always experienced as existing at a time and in a place. The categories of the understanding, he argues, further structure experience, and this enables us to see a world not just in space and time but also built up of parts and wholes, standing in causal relations, and so on. Schopenhauer departs from Kant only a little in this connection, reducing Kant's twelve categories of the understanding to just one, causation. For both thinkers, the world – considered as something which appears to us and which can be known by us – is entirely representational in nature.

For Kant the very notion of a world as it appears to us presupposes something more, namely a reality beyond appearances. Kant and those who follow him operate with a distinction between appearances (phenomena) and things-in-themselves (noumena). Things-in-themselves, Kant argues, are things as they are apart from experience, things which somehow underpin or cause our experience, provide the mind with the raw materials from which a world of objects is constructed. Kant argues that we can know something about appearances, but we can only think haphazardly about things-in-themselves. We cannot say much more about them other than that they exist and interact with the mind in such a way as to cause experience. You might recall that Kant tries to show that the contradictions of speculative metaphysics result from a particular sort of error, namely reason attempting to think outside the world of appearance, trying to bring the categories of the understanding to bear outside the bounds of sensation.

Schopenhauer thinks Kant himself has slipped up here too. Kant maintains that things-in-themselves are somewhere in the causal chain underpinning our experience, but this is to say that the concept of cause applies to something other than or outside of our experience. (You can also wonder what sense might attach to the word 'things' in Kant's expression 'things-in-themselves' – if things get to be things because of the operations of the mind, how could there be *things*-in-themselves?) If Kant is right and the category of cause applies only to objects as they appear, how are we to understand Kant's claim that things-in-themselves do some causing? Schopenhauer argues that another conception of the relation between appearances and things-in-themselves is required, and whatever the relation, it certainly cannot be a causal one.

The world as will

So Schopenhauer needs a different way of thinking about the relationship between the world as it is apart from experience and the experienced world. He claims, courageously, that the world of appearances and the world as it is in itself are the same thing, the same reality, 'viewed' in two different ways. The relationship is not causality; it is identity. On the one hand, the world is representation, but on the other, the world in itself is will. How does he arrive at this intriguing claim? He argues that sensation is not our only access to reality: 'a way from *within* stands open to us to [the] real nature of things'.

There is a sense in which I perceive my body as an object like any other in the physical world. It appears to me in time and space, stands in causal relations, changes over time, and so on. I can and do see it as a representation, an appearance situated in the external, empirical world. But I know about it in another way too. I just saw my hand reach for a glass of juice, but I would have known it was moving even if I had not seen it. Apart from my knowledge of my hand as an object in the world of representations, I have an immediate awareness of it and its movement. I moved my hand intentionally and, as I did so, I also felt a desire for the juice. Of all the objects in the world appearing as representation, I have special access to one of them: my body. I know my body from the inside, as it were, quite apart from my body as a representation, because I inhabit it. On the inside, what I find is will.

It is important to avoid a tempting mistake here. Schopenhauer is not saying that willing causes bodily movements. He has taken Kant to task for thinking that the world as it is in itself helps cause my representations. Instead, Schopenhauer argues that willing is body.

The hand and the will are two aspects of the same reality. In Schopenhauer's language, the hand is 'objectified will'.

Schopenhauer makes a heroic leap from a single window into the hidden side of reality – namely his own access to his body as will – to the claim that the whole world as it appears is nothing but objectified will. Part of the argument depends on a rejection of solipsism, the view that only the self and its representations exist. Schopenhauer also notes that our bodies are parts of the world as it appears, seamlessly integrated into the rest of reality. If I know that the inside of an integrated part is will, why not think of the whole as will too? Once an individual has recognized that his own inner nature is will,

> [h]e will recognize that same will not only in those phenomena that are quite similar to his own, in men and animals, as their innermost nature, but continued reflection will lead him to recognize the force that shoots and vegetates in the plant, indeed the force by which the crystal is formed, the force that turns the magnet . . . all these he will recognize as different only in the phenomenon, but the same according to their inner nature.

The 'way from within' leads Schopenhauer to nothing less than a grasp of what should be beyond the reach of our understanding: the Kantian thing-in-itself.

Now for the bad news. The will is completely devoid of rationality. It is blind and violent striving, mindless and insatiable craving, meaningless impulse. The will has no particular goal or object. It is a simple want which pointlessly drives everything; better, which pointlessly *is* everything. The underlying reality, for Schopenhauer, is a single, unified Cosmic Will – parts, number and the other concepts required to think of things as distinct have no application to the world as it is in itself. In the world as representation, though, the Cosmic Will is fragmented, fractured and struggling against itself. The will 'feasts on itself' in the experienced world, and the feast is terrible, appallingly pointless and painful.

A human life is characterized by nothing but a constant striving after this or that, sometimes momentarily satisfied but more often than not frustrated. On those rare occasions when the will manages to satisfy itself, 'life-benumbing boredom' quickly sets in and the will is reawakened. Life, on Schopenhauer's view, is something which ought not to be, and this is the very worst of all possible worlds. Existence, he says,

> is a constant hurrying of the present into the dead past, a constant dying . . . the life of our body is only a constantly prevented dying, an ever postponed death: finally, in the same way, the activity of our mind is a constantly deferred ennui. Every breath we draw wards off the death that is constantly intruding upon us.

Throwing him out of the salon was probably the right thing to do. Can anything else be done?

Escaping the will

Schopenhauer argues that a temporary escape from the tyranny of willing consists in aesthetic experience. The contemplation of some-thing beautiful snaps us out of the world of representation for a moment, releases us from being subjects striving after objects. If you have a look at a bowl of ripe fruit or a beautiful human body, the will becomes aroused and the awful pattern repeats itself: desire, then either frustration or momentary satisfaction followed by boredom. But if you have a look at a well-executed still life or a finely drawn portrait, the will quietens in a kind of detachment. The object of art is not viewed just as an object categorized by the mind, another desir-able representation. Instead, it is possible to see more than the object, to find oneself in touch with a basic type. Schopenhauer argues that the will manifests itself not only in the particular objects of this world, but also in universal types. These types, Schopenhauer claims, are the Platonic forms themselves, and the artist can communicate her knowledge of them through fine art.

In the moment of aesthetic reverie, the individual passes for a moment beyond simply viewing or hearing a work of art. It is not the particular thing which is contemplated; instead, the individual gains a kind of awareness of something more, a true and basic aspect of reality. In moving past the particular object, she becomes something more than a mere subject. The individual tears herself free from the demands of the will by 'ceasing to be merely individual, and being now a pure will-less subject of knowledge'.

This is, presumably, what we are getting at when we say we 'lose ourselves' in music. There really is a kind of suspension, even peace, which attends the experience of all good art, a feeling of going beyond the thing before us, and perhaps Schopenhauer is on to something here. But he says that through art we are getting in touch with a basic manifestation of the Cosmic Will, and it is hard not to wonder how getting in touch with that terrible thing tears us free of the tyranny of the will itself.

A more lasting escape consists not in aesthetic contemplation, but in ascetic renunciation. When a rare individual genuinely recognizes the world for what it is, sees it as nothing but pointless striving, it is possible for her to free herself in a certain way. Schopenhauer thinks that the path of the morally enlightened individual, the person who tries to love others as she loves herself and do for others as she does for herself, is on the way to seeing the world as it is. What is required is a further step: the individual will turning in on itself. A certain kind of moral thinking can lead a person to the view that self-interest is illusory, and this can evolve into the right sort of renunciation, indifference to all things, self-mortification, self-deprivation – all of this is a deliberate breaking of the will. It results in something much more than a welcome death.

You might want to forgo the fasting, flagellation and hair shirts and go straight for suicide, but Schopenhauer argues that this would be a mistake. Suicide is self-defeating, an affirmation of the will, a recognition that the sorrow of life matters. A life which ends as a consequence of the denial of the will, Schopenhauer maintains, ends differently. Suicide merely destroys an individual in the world as representation, but the death of the saint, he hints, has an effect on the thing-in-itself, somehow breaks the noumenal will. Schopenhauer cites Eastern philosophy regularly in his consideration of the denial of the will, and whatever he might mean by the extinction of the will through acetic denial, it has something to do with the nothingness of nirvana. But pointing to this obscure doctrine is not much help if we are after an understanding of Schopenhauer's meaning here. What is left when the will is denied in the right way? What is nothing?

Schopenhauer has something of an answer to this. He argues that there is not a great deal positive which can be said about nothing. We cannot say anything positive because we cannot really know anything about nothing. Knowing requires a subject and an object known, and Schopenhauer is talking about the abolition of subject, object, space, time, understanding and the will itself. He can only point us to nirvana and similar, mystical talk of 'ecstasy, rapture, illumination, union with God, and so on'. If he cannot offer a positive account of nothing, perhaps predictably he has a go at negativity, at saying what nothing is not. As he puts it, perhaps too succinctly: 'No will: no representation, no world.' If there is any happiness at all in Schopenhauer's writings, you can hear the slightest murmur of it when he considers nothing, even if he has nothing positive to say about it: 'to those in whom the will has turned and denied itself, this very real world of ours with all its suns and galaxies is – nothing'.

13 The Communist Manifesto

Karl Marx (1818–83)

The Communist Manifesto is short, sharp, clear and visionary. It has inspired generations of militants, political agitators, and many others of a less revolutionary bent. The book usually has both Marx and Friedrich Engels listed as authors, but it is clear that Marx drafted the bulk of it. Engels himself said that the book is 'essentially Marx's work'. We will refer only to Marx in what follows.

In order to understand the content and ambition of the *Manifesto* it is important to think a little about the times in which Marx wrote it. 1848 was a year of revolutionary upheaval. There were worker uprisings and revolts in the major industrial areas of Northern Europe. Working class discontent was in the air and something dramatic was expected to develop from the ferment of revolutionary activity. 'A spectre is haunting Europe', Marx writes, 'and that spectre is communism'. Communism is a power, he thought, and it was high time that the power had a coherent voice; this, anyway, was only part of Marx's aim in writing the *Manifesto*. His other aim was to change the world by hurrying it on to its last historical phase: communism. You can smell more than a whiff of Hegel here, and clearly Marx's historical materialism is a reworking of Hegel's conception of the Absolute becoming self-conscious in the phases of history. Instead of the Absolute realizing itself in history, Marx hopes that the working classes will realize their power. And use it.

Marx was commissioned to write a mission statement by the League of Communists. They were after a clear expression of their political goals to provide the focus for an expected revolution and its aftermath. Marx wrote the *Manifesto* in around six weeks, with drafts going back and forth between Engels and other supporters. Very few of those drafts survive, and many take this as evidence for the fact that Marx made few changes or adjustments to his original vision. No matter how it arose, the *Manifesto* is one of the most famous works of political philosophy.

It contains a summary of Marx's own philosophy of historical materialism, which was set out at great length by Marx and Engels in an earlier unpublished work, *The German Ideology*. The *Manifesto* also contains a strikingly prophetic vision about the future of capitalism. We will have a look at Marx's conception of history, his treatment of other forms of socialism, and finally glance at the work's prophetic content.

Historical materialism

The *Manifesto* contains a philosophy of history, what has come to be known as historical materialism. According to this view, and in line with Hegel, there is a pattern or shape to human history, and history is heading towards an end point. The end or goal is not, as Hegel would have it, an awareness of the process, but a certain sort of economic organization: communism. Before society is ready for communism, though, it must pass through certain stages of economic and social development. A large part of the book is a treatment of these stages, with a kind of hope that present workers who see the stages for what they are will do something about the current stage, namely change it. Marx is fomenting an historical push, and the book is meant to help history along.

Marx's theory of history does not attempt to explain human history as such, but account for the evolution of a part of it, namely our economic and social history. Marx's view begins with the claim that before any human collective can do or achieve anything worth achieving, individuals must be able to meet their fundamental material needs. Before all else, a person needs to eat, have clothing and have some sort of shelter from the elements. Societies and civilizations rely on particular 'modes of production' to secure the basic needs of living. In chapter one of the *Manifesto*, Marx sets out his view that the history of European civilization is characterized by progress from the ancient mode of production to the feudal mode, and from the feudal mode to the capitalist mode of production.

Marx argues that humans in pre-history simply foraged for their material requirements. They ate whatever animals and vegetation they found lying around; they used fur from the animals they devoured in order to clothe themselves; they sheltered in natural caves. According to Marx, human history proper started when humans actually produced things to meet their needs, rather than simply taking whatever nature served them. Particularly, human beings began to cultivate land in order to grow crops and build pens to rear animals for meat and fur. We began quarrying stone and chopping down trees in order to build huts and eventually villages.

With the beginnings of something like a civilized life, though, came social strata, the creation of unequal classes. Marx maintains that every productive set-up produces not just stuff, but a ruling class and a working class. The working class produces the stuff needed to survive, and the ruling class stands over them, appropriating the surplus of their labour. The workers, then, are always somehow exploited by the ruling class for the latter's own material needs and, ultimately, their excesses.

The earliest European modes of production dominated life in Ancient Egypt, Greece and Rome. Marx calls this epoch the 'ancient mode of production'. Here a class of masters has slave labour at its disposal. Other workers – craftsmen, artists, musicians, and so on – simply get plugged in around the basic economic relationship between the master and the slave. For example, the master trades part of the surplus produce of his slaves for the entertainment provided by his excellent dancing troupe and fine musicians. Throughout it all, it is the basic economic relationship which defines the times. The slave is the one producing what everyone else really requires, namely the necessities of food, clothing and shelter.

The feudal mode of production is next in line. Here the landed serf rather than the homebound slave produces the material needs of society. The serf enjoys a fractionally greater freedom than that of his enslaved predecessors. Serfs have some property rights which actually matter, namely the use of land, as well as a degree of power in determining when and how they deploy their labour. Still, Marx notes, the land that serfs labour on is not really theirs; it is owned by the lords of the manor and, ultimately, by the monarch. The ruling classes demand a rent for the use of their land. In this way they appropriate the surplus production of serfs in order to provide for their own material needs and, it nearly goes without saying, their many excesses.

Marx argues that the feudal mode of production eventually gives way to the capitalist mode of production. Here wage-labourers, or the proletariat, become the main workers in society. The class of capitalists, not slave masters or feudal lords, stands over the working class, as the ruling class always has. The capitalist class exploits the proletariat and appropriates the surplus of their labour, now through the instruments of profit-making. Profit provides capitalists with the money for their own consumption, particularly their consumption of luxuries, as well as the money to invest in and control society's means of production. Money is now a way to make more money.

Part of the ambition of Marx's historical materialism is to reveal the economic workings of all societies. Another ambition, no doubt his principal one, is agitation for change, to push the inevitable course of human history along a little more quickly. The *Manifesto*, then, is a summary of Marx's historical materialism, a series of snapshots along the evolutionary road to the capitalist present. It is an argument for just one claim: the 'history of all hitherto existing societies is a history of class struggle'. Once you see history in terms of class struggle, Marx argues, your eyes are opened and you should want to do something about it. You should want to do something about it particularly if you are on the side of the worker, who by now looks like the present analogue of the slave or the serf.

Marx believes that once members of the working class become conscious of their own interests and their condition of exploitation by the ruling capitalist class, then they will inevitably rise up and bring forth a revolution which would lead to a society in which working-class interests would be better served. The worker uprisings of 1848 had already demonstrated that the proletarian class had a glimmering of the required sort of consciousness and were on the way to realizing that their interests in life were being frustrated by the capitalist order and the economic system. The *Manifesto* is Marx's attempt to locate their vague hopes for social transformation in a story about the shape and final destiny of human history.

In the *Manifesto*, Marx anchors revolutionary proletarian ambitions in historical materialism, and this is a large break with the socialist thinking which came before him. The historical connection gets a large hearing and is the main point of the work's first two chapters. Chapter two also includes Marx's responses to anticipated bourgeois capitalist objections to the coming age of communism. In chapters three and four Marx changes tack and criticizes other socialist responses to the plight of proletarians in capitalist society.

Socialism before Marx was a simple but amorphous reaction to the evil effects of capitalism on human life. Socialist thinkers were generally horrified at how human beings were being forced to work and live, but the horror was directed at small-scale sorts of change. Socialist movements arose in order to improve the condition of workers in the face of capitalism but, for Marx, much more than minor changes were required. His fundamental objection to other sorts of socialist thinking is put in a medical metaphor. First, they fail to come to a complete diagnosis of the problem of life as a proletarian and, second, they fail to advance a suitable cure for this horrible condition.

Critique of socialism

So Marx takes up and criticizes three forms of socialism. Reactionary socialists think that we can and should undo the miserable effect of capitalism by simply going back to our feudal past. They claim that we were better off under feudalism and that the new capitalist order is a step backwards. Marx in no way wanted to downplay the misery which capitalism visits upon people; however, he argues that capitalism is some sort of advance on feudalism. Given his commitment to historical materialism, he has to think of it this way. So what you find is Marx chastising reactionary socialists for their 'total incapacity to comprehend the march of modern history'. For Marx, capitalism delivers suffering but it also engenders the economic and political means of salvation from such suffering. It is a kind of step forward, so steps backwards are, for him, no help at all.

Marx also criticizes bourgeois socialists. These are socialists who can see the advantages that capitalism has brought to human society but think that its negative effects can be ameliorated in some way to make capitalism more palatable. Bourgeois socialists believe that capitalist society can be a steady, stable and harmonious form of economic organization if the rough edges are softened through socialist-minded reform. Marx rejects this version of socialism because, among other things, capitalism is a fundamentally class-ridden economic system. Where there are classes, there is a conflict of interests and, inevitably, exploitation. Conflict of interest and exploitation cannot just be finessed away, and, certainly, a society with exploitation in it cannot be stable or harmonious.

Marx also attacks variations on utopian socialism. Such socialists might be well-meaning, he argues, but their solutions to the workers' plight are naive. Utopian socialists certainly recognize the suffering of a capitalist system, but their blueprints for a happier society are, by Marx's lights, not radical enough and, possibly, rooted in a conception of human nature which is too good to be true. Utopian socialists such as Robert Owen conducted small-scale experiments in socialist living which he thought could simply be spread throughout an industrial economy. There was, Marx thought, no chance of this as long as the means of production were in the hands of capitalists.

According to Marx, what is fundamentally wrong with all three sorts of socialists is a general failure to perceive the revolutionary potential of the growing mass of proletarians in capitalist society. If society is to improve, if the lives of the working classes are to get any better, the transformation of society will have to be radical. What's needed is revolution. The *Manifesto* can be read as nothing less than a lesson in history for the proletariat, an attempt to make them see their power and their historical destiny. The ultimate aim, as always for Marx, is to speed humanity closer to a better world.

Marx expected revolution from the proletariat. The *Manifesto* is imbued with that expectation and openly declares it. As noted at the start, the *Manifesto* reflects the time of its writing: 1848 was a year of revolutionary upheaval in the centres of capitalist industry in Europe. However, those revolutions eventually came to nothing and by 1849 had fizzled out. The course of capitalist development since Marx has led to the decline of traditional working-class and socialist movements. The proletariat never emerged, globally, as the agent for dramatic social change as Marx anticipated in the *Manifesto*. His prophecy really was falsified by subsequent history. However, there are other prophecies in the *Manifesto* which do seem to be confirmed by the course of history.

Other prophecies

The *Manifesto* does anticipate the spread of capitalism throughout the globe and the development of a 'world market' for goods and labour. Marx argued that no society on the planet will be left untouched by the reach of capitalism, and he was right about that. Indeed, Marx can be considered one of the first theorists of what is now called 'globalization'. Marx also anticipates the development of societies in which the small-mindedness of village life is dwarfed by the cosmopolitanism and internationalism of city-based life. Marx also saw the loss of traditionally secure and well-paid middle-class occupations and the rise and spread of the 'proletarianization' of professional work. Many think that these predictions have come true, and probably a lot of people think the world is worse for it.

Marx also anticipated a decline in the power of nationalist and religious thought, but, as we have witnessed in the twentieth century and at the unpleasant start of this millennium, wars stoked by nationalism and religion still seem to dominate human affairs. You can share Marx's hope that we will progress into a time without the fictions and irrationalities of nationalism and religion, but it is clear that we are not there yet.

New marxists

The failure of the proletariat to perform the historical role which Marx anticipated for them in the *Manifesto* has led many to reject Marx's thinking. Some say that this is too quick. Maybe it is the case that the philosophy underpinning historical materialism is true and that Marx just got the timing wrong. The urgency of the time in which Marx wrote the *Manifesto* might have fuelled this mistake, if that is what it is. Still others maintain that Marx got the timing right, but object to the so-called fruits of communism. Many of Marx's predictions have come to pass, in the former Soviet Union, China and elsewhere, but communism in such places has resulted in a great deal of suffering and death. You can object to Marx on ethical grounds and leave quibbles about historical accuracy to others.

Some move on from the particulars of Marx, take lessons from history, and still hope for other kinds of revolutionary means which could secure a better world. Some see simple truths in Marx's historical materialism. They buy into the Marxist view that human beings exchange master–slave relations for lord–serf relations because of the improved productivity which these new relations promise. The lord–serf relationship grew and proliferated because it was better able to satisfy human needs and wants. Similarly, capitalist–worker relations arose because of the greater productivity which they delivered over the lord–serf relationship. But the final move, from capitalism to what New Marxists call 'true communism', has not been made. You can keep the story but drop Marx's insistence that then was the time for revolution. Maybe it is now.

Critics of capitalism, many with Marx in mind, note that capitalism need not be thought of as the summit of human history. They argue that it is not a steady, stable and harmonious economic system. Capitalism might deliver many advantages, they concede, but it brings with it a large share of frustration and misery. As long as this is true, Marx will be relevant for us, they claim. The *Manifesto* provides us with an account of the human condition and it points to a solution to the problems we face in the part of our lives which depend on economics. It provides a model which suggests a way to refine our views of the problems and the solutions we might want to try in order to deliver a better world. In this, for many, lies the enduring relevance of *The Communist Manifesto.*

14 Utilitarianism
John Stuart Mill (1806–73)

Utilitarianism is the view that the moral rightness or wrongness of an act depends on the consequences of the act for human happiness. You can find expressions of the view in Priestly and Locke, but its most famous defenders are Jeremy Bentham and John Stuart Mill. Reasonable people can disagree about whose treatment is best, and you might be annoyed to see that Mill's book, not Bentham's *An Introduction to the Principles of Morals and Legislation*, gets star billing here. Mill, you might think, is only reworking and correcting Bentham's earlier insights. A case could be made, though, for the claim that Mill takes the view further, and his account does have more meat on the bones than the version appearing in Bentham's book. If it makes you feel any better, we will consider Bentham's treatment in some detail first.

It is hard, anyway, to have anything but genuine affection for someone like Bentham, and leaving him out of a consideration of Mill is not just an intellectual error; it feels wrong. Bentham is just too remarkable to ignore. In addition to his work in philosophy and legal theory, he designed portable houses, heating systems and refrigeration units, counterfeit-proof bank notes, plans for the freezing of peas, and the infamous Panopticon, a prison designed to keep inmates under the constant surveillance of only a few guards. He coined a stupefying number of words too – 'maximize', 'minimize', 'rationale', 'demoralize', 'unilateral', 'detachable', 'exhaustive' and 'international' among them. We can look away from 'catastatico-chrestic physiurgics', which, sadly, never caught on. He also made arrangements to have his body stuffed, mounted and put on display, allegedly to serve as a visual inspiration to his followers after his departure from this earth. The autoicon, as it is called, is still on view in a corner of University College London. His followers, the Philosophical Radicals, proposed changes to the law on the treatment of animals, homosexuality, suffrage, property, taxation and much else, changing lives for the better because of his principles. Bentham was clearly excellent in many respects. How could someone like this possibly be left out of an account of the nature of happiness?

The greatest happiness principle

Bentham's large contribution to philosophy is his attempt to place rationality at the heart of morality and legislation. The punishments recommended by the law of his day seemed grounded not in rational principle, but in falsehoods and fictions. In particular, the severity of a given punishment seemed to be a function of nothing more than the offence the crime caused in the hearts of lawmakers. Further, he argues that the words 'ought', 'right' and 'wrong' have no clear meaning, certainly no clear and rational expression in law. He cuts through the absurdities and prejudices underpinning legal complexity and the confusions of moral language with a single principle: the principle of utility or the greatest happiness principle.

He says very clearly what he means by the principle: it 'approves or disapproves of every action whatsoever, according to the tendency which it appears to have to augment or diminish the happiness of the part whose interest is in question'. The principle, and the conception of happiness on which it depends, is based on human nature. Human beings, Bentham argues, are governed by two masters: pleasure and pain. Increasing an individual human's happiness is nothing less than increasing the balance of pleasure over pain in her life. Increasing human happiness in a society, therefore, is a matter of increasing the general balance of pleasure over pain in the community. Morality falls out of all of this just as quickly. Any action which conforms to the principle of utility, which augments the overall balance of pleasure over pain, ought to be done: it is morally right.

The hedonistic calculus

You might already be wondering how pleasures and pains are to be balanced or weighed up. If alternative courses of action present themselves to me, how on earth do I decide which augments the happiness on the part of those whose interest is in question? How much pleasure results from donating some money to charity as compared to spending the money on a festive lunch for me and a few friends? Pleasures and pains just do not seem like the sorts of things which admit of quantification. Is the pleasure attending our full stomachs worth less than the elimination of a little pain in Africa? Bentham's answer is to propose a decision procedure called 'the hedonistic calculus'. Not only are pleasure and pain quantifiable, but he formulates a system for their quantification.

The following factors, he argues, should figure into the calculation: the intensity, duration, certainty, propinquity, fecundity, purity and extent of the pleasure or pain. You then consider the persons whose interests seem most affected, and reflect on the immediate pleasures or pains which result, as well as the pleasures and pains which quickly follow. Bentham, slide-rule in hand, says that you must then, '[s]um up all the values of all the *pleasures* on the one side, and those of all the pains on the other. The balance, if it be on the side of pleasure, will give the *good* tendency of the act upon the whole . . .'

Even this short sketch of Bentham's views suggests some difficulties. We will focus on a few which Mill addresses in *Utilitarianism*, and we will also have a look at his disastrous proof of Bentham's principle.

Mill considers the objection that the doctrine of utilitarianism is somehow degrading, not worth the name 'moral theory', because it is a species of hedonism. Hedonism comes in many flavours, but all versions share the claim that pleasure is good, if not the supreme good. Certainly Mill's characterization of utilitarianism fits the mould: 'the greatest happiness principle holds that actions are right in proportion as they tend to promote happiness, wrong as they tend to produce the reverse of happiness. By "happiness" is intended pleasure, and the absence of pain . . .' As Bentham argued before him, then, Mill maintains that actions are right just insofar as they produce pleasure. This is hedonism, if anything is. You can wonder, as some of Bentham's detractors did, how the desire for pleasure could inform morality. Isn't morality in the business of teaching us to choose what is right, not simply what feels good? We were going to choose what feels good anyway, if left to our own devices, and what is needed from a moral code is something which helps us occasionally to look beyond pleasure towards something higher, more exalted – something noble. Isn't the utilitarian suggesting a beastly life of maximized pleasure, a life fit for a pig but not a human being?

The quality of pleasure

The response Mill gives is perhaps his largest and most interesting departure from Bentham's views. He points out that it is not the utilitarian whose conception of pleasure and happiness is degrading. Instead, the objection itself depends on a degrading representation of human nature and the pleasures of which we are capable. The objection supposes that the sort of pleasure human beings can enjoy is nothing more than base or beastly pleasures. This is to overlook the quality of pleasures, to fail to distinguish between higher and lower pleasures. Bentham got himself into trouble by suggesting that poetry is no more valuable than the simple-minded game of Pushpin from the point of view of calculating pleasure. Mill argues that the quantity of pleasure is not the only factor which must figure in our reflections on what is right: the quality of the pleasure matters too. Certainly we are capable of experiencing beastly pleasures, but pleasures of a higher quality are possible as well. The objection, and perhaps Bentham's earlier formulation of utilitarianism, misses this distinction.

How can you tell whether one pleasure is qualitatively better than another? Mill claims that someone who has experienced both higher and lower pleasures will generally prefer the former, no matter what quantities are involved. For example, if you have experienced both backrubs and Bach, you will have a marked preference for Bach. Mill, apparently standing atop a stump, points out that

> It is better to be a human being dissatisfied than a pig satisfied; better to be
> Socrates dissatisfied than a fool satisfied. And if the fool, or the pig, are of a
> different opinion, it is because they only know their side of the question.

Not only is there a marked difference between the two sorts of pleasures, but the higher ones are also of such a quality that no quantity of the lower can match them.

Well, on some mornings, I just don't know. Pigs look fairly happy, and, if we are supposed to maximize happiness, shouldn't the utilitarian urge us to join the swine in the filthy mud and submerge ourselves in beastly pleasures? Such pleasures are easier to come by and, anyway, why take the risk of dissatisfaction associated with trying to live the elevated life of the aesthete? Mill's answer seems to be that once you have had and fully appreciated both kinds of pleasure, you will prefer higher to lower ones. But if the right thing to do is to maximize pleasure, this alleged preference is beside the point. Even if everyone in fact prefers higher pleasures, doesn't the principle of utility counsel that we should aim for whatever pleasure we can get? Would it not therefore be better to be a pig satisfied?

It might be that this reaction misses part of the point of utilitarianism, namely the claim that it is not just my pleasures which should concern me, but the happiness of everyone affected by my actions. We should not be thinking in terms of our own little pig sties, but of the happiness of the community itself. Mill hints that a few miserable intellectuals are a small price to pay for a culture in which it is possible to experience higher pleasures. But the claim that individuals must be concerned with the happiness of everyone suggests another set of difficulties.

Further objections to the view

The level of disinterestedness required to be a good utilitarian might be too much for anyone to achieve. Is it really possible for me to forget the fact that some of the people affected by my actions are near and dear to me, friends and family and lovers? Can an individual really sum up pleasures and pains, without a thought for who is feeling those pleasures and pains? Utilitarianism seems to be telling us to be more than a little cold and unsympathizing in our calculations. If morality leads us anywhere, you might think, it should lead us in the opposite direction.

In reply to the first charge – that utilitarianism expects too much of us, that we simply cannot achieve the level of disinterestedness it recommends – Mill argues that the motives underpinning moral choice can in practice be as varied as you like; what matters are the consequences. A person might rescue a drowning baby because she believes in the general sanctity of human life or because she hopes for a reward. What matters is that she undertook the action, that the right consequences were brought about, not her motives or the level of interest she in fact had in the child. Whether she jumped in to save her own baby or someone else's baby is beside the point: what matters is that the baby is rescued. Our being interested in each other's welfare is compatible with the view that the consequences, not the motives, matter in the moral evaluation of action. After all, it is happiness for all that we are after. The focus for purposes of moral evaluation might be on consequences, but our focus in acting can sometimes be elsewhere.

In reply to the second complaint – that utilitarianism chills our feelings towards individuals, makes us consider just the consequences of actions and not the people who act – Mill argues that other things besides the consequences of actions can and do matter to us. Some people have good or bad characters, some are brave or wise or benevolent, and all of this is a part of our estimation of them as persons, but not our estimation of the moral worth of their actions. Utilitarianism, again, is compatible with this part of our moral lives. There is no inconsistency in saying that facts about more than the consequences of action matter to us.

The disastrous proof

Following a consideration of these and other objections, Mill formulates what he calls a 'proof' of the principle of utility, and philosophers have wondered about its status ever since. It is not entirely clear what Mill is up to in this part of the book. Just what is he trying to prove? You might think of him as arguing as follows. Utilitarianism holds that pleasure has a particular sort of value: it is the pleasure caused by an act which renders that act morally good. What proof do we have that pleasure has this special value, a value with a moral consequence? Why think pleasure is something we ought to pursue as an end, even as the supreme end? Mill writes: 'The sole evidence it is possible to produce that anything is desirable, is that people do actually desire it. If the end which the utilitarian doctrine proposes to itself were not, in theory and in practice, acknowledged to be an end, nothing could ever convince any person that it was so'.

Mill seems to argue that pleasure really is desired by everyone, so it is, therefore, desirable. But does this make pleasure valuable in the way required of a moral system? All Mill has shown, if he has shown anything, is that pleasure is in fact desired, but this cannot be enough to get him to the conclusion that pleasure ought to be desired. Talking about facts will only tell us what is so, not what ought to be so. It looks like his conclusion needs an 'ought' in it, but only manages an 'is'.

The argument looks a lot worse if you reflect further on Mill's talk of desirability. He says that the only things visible are things seen; the only things audible are things heard. Similarly, he seems to argue that the only things desirable are things desired – and what everyone desires is pleasure. So pleasure is desirable. Does the analogy work? Visible things are not just things seen, but things which can be seen. Audible things are things which can be heard. Certainly what people desire is whatever can be desired. But saying that pleasure can be desired is not the same thing as saying pleasure is desirable. Mill is only entitled to the lesser claim (pleasure can be desired), and he needs the stronger one (pleasure is desirable) for his argument to work.

Is it, anyway, even true that people desire pleasure first and foremost? Mill's argument presupposes that when I desire something, what I desire is the pleasure which attends getting that something. When I desire a beer, what I really desire is the pleasure which comes along with having a beer. But sometimes, or so it can seem, what I really want is a beer, not the pleasure I get from drinking it. If you talk yourself into the view that pleasure is really only a secondary thing, you can start thinking that what we desire is a very mixed and complex bag and that pleasure and pain only figure into our psychology from time to time. This would be bad for utilitarianism, holding as it does that seeking pleasure and avoiding pain are, as Bentham puts it, our two masters.

Justice

There is a final worry which is much harder for utilitarians to deal with, and it has something to do with justice. Suppose our community is suffering from a great deal of pain in the form of insecurity. Perhaps a string of violent murders has been committed, and no one among us feels safe enough to sleep or go out at night. There is a lot more pain than pleasure in our many lives. Maybe our law enforcement officials do a little hedonistic calculus, and come to the conclusion that stitching up an innocent scapegoat will calm our fears. Maybe it will put the real criminal off. Anyway, punishing someone they know is innocent will only cause comparatively little pain in the form of a single ruined life. If they handle it well, no one will ever find out. Maybe they can pick someone who annoys the rest of us: putting him away would do a lot of good. Perhaps, on reflection, killing him by painless injection would remove whatever pain his suffering in prison might add to the ledger. The rest of us can get on with racking up our pleasures. Does utilitarianism not only condone what looks like a monstrously immoral act, but also recommend it, call it morally right?

There is a hard bullet to bite here. Some maintain that the scape-goat is a good idea. If our moral intuitions suggest otherwise, so much the worse for them. Utilitarianism's insight has to do with what matters to us, the consequences of action for human happiness, not something as wishy-washy as lofty intentions. But unless the inten-tions and the consequences match up some of the time, you might conclude that the happiness secured is somehow undeserved.

15   Thus Spoke Zarathustra
Friedrich Nietzsche (1844–1900)

Nietzsche occupies the strange position on the Venn Diagram of Philosophers at the intersection of the areas picking out those who are German, unconventional, influential, outrageous, difficult and incredibly readable. He is all of these things, but it is the fact that he is an excellent stylist which explains a large part of Nietzsche's continuing attraction. No one would change a word of it, but the prose can get in the way of the philosophy, readable though it is. Nietzsche does not always give an argument for his conclusions, nor does he put those conclusions in the clearest possible language. He seems to have a penchant for shocking turns of phrase, and this too can get in the way of coming to an understanding of him. His writing is also open to many interpretations, and this is a consequence he no doubt had in mind. All of this is at least partly explained by Nietzsche's view that our fascination with truth is a kind of illness which is itself in need of investigation. There are no facts on Nietzsche's view. Instead there are as many interpretations as there are creative people, and the right thing to do is to try out as many interpretations as possible as a kind of experiment.

His conclusions are, anyway, almost always provocative, and Nietzsche claims that *Thus Spoke Zarathustra* contains the whole of his philosophy – all of his conclusions, or perhaps interpretations, such as they are. Nietzsche ranges widely in the book, as you might expect, but we will focus on just the largest parts of it: his attack on Christianity, the will to power, the Superman, and the doctrine of eternal return. This is a lot to manage in a short space, but the ideas are interconnected, and it is hard to understand just a part of it without some grip on the rest.

The book begins with Zarathustra, a kind of prophet, in meditation at the top of a mountain. He has spent ten years in seclusion and reflection, with only his eagle, a symbol of pride, and his serpent, a symbol of wisdom, for company. He decides to come down from the mountain and teach the wisdom he has managed to acquire. Zarathustra encounters a saint, various townspeople, a tightrope walker, and finally a donkey that seems to be the object of worship by a few confused and lowly people. Zarathustra talks sometimes to those around him but often to himself but, no matter who he encounters, no one is ready for his news.

The first part of the book makes the claim that individuals can expect no help from God or the supernatural in this life; in a literal sense, our destinies are in our own hands. Part two begins Nietzsche's treatment of the Superman, as well as the will to power. Part three includes a discussion of the eternal return. Part four, which Nietzsche did not intend to be the last part of the book, takes up the possibility of accepting only a part of the teaching of Zarathustra. Obviously, for Nietzsche, that will not do. We will start, as Nietzsche does, with his attack on religion generally and Christianity in particular.

Christianity

In a letter to his friend Franz Overbeck, Nietzsche says that what is most distinctive in *Zarathustra* is its treatment of Christianity: 'there has not been since Voltaire such an outrageous attack on Christianity – and, to tell the truth, even Voltaire had no idea that one could attack it in this way'. Seeing the outrage for what it is depends on knowing something about Nietzsche's conception of value. Nietzsche is sometimes mistaken for a straightforward nihilist, one who holds that values have no justification or meaning. You can find in Nietzsche's writings the claim that there are no standards of morality, that truth is meaningless, that religion is dead or at best dying; but nihilism is his starting point, not his conclusion. Nietzsche argues that the West's intellectual and interpretive scaffolding, the underlying concepts which we use to arrive at judgements of value, can no longer sustain us. Maybe once we could buy into the notion that value is rooted in something other-worldly, but now we have wised up, and religion is no longer enough. Nietzsche is worried that we are on the cusp of a crisis of value, and we will have to fill in the spiritual blanks ourselves in order to survive.

For Nietzsche, then, human beings create value in the universe, and this creative possibility is at the heart of things for him, because values and the manner in which we rank them determines our perspective on everything. Although gods were thought to be the source of value, gods themselves are just the product of our creative nature. 'God is dead', Nietzsche claims, and by this he means that a certain sort of comfy metaphysics has outlived its usefulness to us, is no longer necessary or good for human life. Focusing on God or worrying about the afterlife is bothering about nothing, turning away from what might matter, namely this life and what we manage to make of it. What is needed is something else, and that something else, whatever it is, cannot be handed to us by a priest. We will have to work it out ourselves.

You can arrive at some conception of Nietzsche's understanding of value by considering his thoughts on master and slave morality, which he explores in *Beyond Good and Evil* and *Genealogy of Morals*. Nietzsche argues that morality falls into two fundamental types: master morality and slave morality. The former is an ancient conception of value, in which the strong or powerful engage in moral talk as a kind of self-affirmation. The strong call their own qualities 'good', and consider the qualities of the weak 'bad'. Thus, according to master morality, strength, power, control and self-determination are good, and weakness, sickness, impotence and the generally bovine qualities of the herd are bad. The powerless, in an act Nietzsche regards as deeply repugnant, have somehow managed to invert master morality in what Nietzsche calls a kind of 'slave revolt'. The weak have turned the moral equation around. According to the morality of slaves, the weak, meek, and powerless alone are good, as manifested dramatically by a suffering God on the cross. The qualities of the strong are regarded as not just bad, but evil, deserving of divine punishment. With the rise of Christianity and the fall of the Greek and Roman celebration of strength, power and individualism, humanity has become something contemptible. By celebrating weakness, we have devolved into something unspeakable, for

Nietzsche, something which must be overcome. Far from arguing for nihilism, Nietzsche is calling for something akin to a return to pre-Christian values.

The Superman and willing

But he is not suggesting that we simply ape the Ancients. Value is something we must seek for ourselves, but where do we look? The answer has something to do with humanity, but not much. For Nietzsche, human beings are not valuable in themselves, particularly in their current, servile state. Instead, the value of humanity consists in being a means to a higher type of man, what he calls the '*Übermensch*' – Overman or Superman. As Zarathustra says, 'Man is a rope, fastened between beast and Superman – a rope over an abyss . . . What is great in man is that he is a bridge and not a goal . . .' The point of human beings, what Nietzsche hopes might save us from the crisis of value, is that we might become something better, a higher kind of being. Zarathustra's aim is to teach just this:

> Man is something that should be overcome . . . You have made your way from worm to man, and much in you is still worm . . . Behold, I teach you the Superman. The Superman is the meaning of the earth. Let your will say: The Superman shall be the meaning of the earth.

What is the Superman? Nietzsche says rather a lot about what it is not. He discusses a number of sorts of escape, ways in which human beings deliberately avoid the question of value in their lives. We sleep, literally and metaphorically, and in so doing make our lives a kind of death. We have also fallen into the religious injunction to love the soul and renounce the body, and in doing this we turn away from the only lives we shall ever have. We fall under the control of the state, and thus give up on the chance to make choices for ourselves, decide what matters to us. There is some discussion here and elsewhere in Nietzsche's writings of the many excellences associated with war. We have come to love peace, he says, but war brings out our best qualities. The Superman, anyway, will not be a sleeper. He will delight in the body, make his own choices, revel in war and, above all, assert his will.

The will to power appears almost everywhere in Nietzsche, initially as a force underlying some human choices but eventually as something underpinning or driving everything. You can here more than a murmur of Schopenhauer in here, and certainly Nietzsche was heavily influenced by him. However, Nietzsche rejects Schopenhauer's pessimistic conclusions by arguing that the will is not merely a blind impulse. Nietzsche claims that the will is after something in particular, namely power. Instead of following Schopenhauer's partial recommendation that one ought to try to break the will by denying it, Nietzsche urges us to embrace the will. The Superman will do just this.

Recall the slave revolt in morality. The slaves, by inverting the values of the strong, were expressing the will to power in a way, but it amounted to the will turning in on itself, like a caged beast gnawing at its own flesh. The Superman, a free spirit, will express the will to power in its purest or highest form, will seek out challenges, danger, and opportunities for self-affirmation. The Superman, in short, is one who affirms his will without compromise.

You can get the feeling that Nietzsche is thinking of something like a powerful aristocrat in his emphasis on the Superman. The conception is not racist, as is sometimes thought, but it is elitist. The Superman cares only for himself, his own causes, and possibly his equals. Who else could be worth his concern? Everyone and everything else is fodder for his enterprises. This is not selfishness, but right thinking, according to Nietzsche. The Superman sees value in himself and his agenda and, in doing this, is a kind of master of what matters most: value itself. Nietzsche might object to the comparison, but it can help us to get a handle on the notion.

The eternal return

You can also find something like advice about the sort of self-affirmation exhibited by the Superman by considering Nietzsche's doctrine of the eternal return. It first appears in aphorism 341 of *The Gay Science*, but it gets a much larger hearing in *Zarathustra*. You can find your way into it by thinking of it as something of a thought experiment. Suppose you discover that you are to live your life exactly as you already have, over and over and over again for eternity. Each choice, each mistake, each regret, each happiness and all the rest must be lived by you in an eternally repeating cycle. For ever. Now think about your reaction to this news. Does the thought fill you with joy? Would you be horrified at the prospect of having to endure it all over again (and again and again) for all of eternity? For Nietzsche, if you are filled with joy at the prospect, you are at least nearer the end of the bridge towards the Superman than one who reacts with horror. Zarathustra, for his part, has some difficulty in accepting the possibility that not just the best returns but the worst of humanity returns too. He stomachs it eventually.

In his autobiography Nietzsche describes the doctrine of the eternal return as the highest expression of affirmation that one can possibly attain and regards it as the foundation of the whole of *Zarathustra*. There is, however, at least the possibility that Nietzsche took the doctrine literally, as a truth about the nature of reality. Certainly his later notebooks suggest just this. It is hard to say, as both his autobiography and his notebooks were written quite close to Nietzsche's descent into insanity. We can leave it for others to decide, and settle here for just the weaker notion that the doctrine has something to do with the nature of willing, not metaphysics.

Evaluating Nietzsche

Is there anything true in all of this? This is a question which might not be fair, given Nietzsche's conception of truth and talk of interpretation and perspective, but we need to ask it anyway. Nietzsche certainly is a cultural critic of great profundity, and if literary skill here is a measure of truth, then certainly there is truth in Nietzsche. He really is on to something when he notices that our conception of value is, or anyway was, undergoing a kind of crisis. It is possible that we have solved it or possibly put it on hold for a while, no doubt in a manner Nietzsche would have found appalling. Probably he is right in thinking that religion cannot keep us moderns afloat much longer. Maybe it is true that we can avert the worst of the crisis by looking to the clear-sighted creation of value ourselves. One question which arises in this connection is, roughly: Is Nietzsche's solution the best one? Are the values he puts to the fore the right ones?

Nietzsche advocates the rise of the Superman as the right response to the death of God, and the accompanying ethic is not exactly pleasant, nor is it meant to be. The worth of humanity, if Nietzsche has it right, is to give way to something most of us would regard as terrible. The free man, Nietzsche tells us, is above all a warrior, a conqueror, one who grinds the weak underfoot in the service of his own aims. Do we have to countenance that horror in order to escape the horrors of nihilism?

Certainly there is a reply to all of this in Nietzsche, and it is to point out that our worries about the Superman in particular and Nietzsche's treatment of the problem of value in general, though well founded, are the result of our own weakness. We are all still part of the herd, the weak, the many and, as Zarathustra himself discovered, we are not yet ready for Nietzsche's teachings. Well, all right, but there is something dubious about this move. Certainly Nietzsche's ethic is self-consistent, but do we not require more from philosophy?

This objection or question is certainly some distance from one which appears all too frequently in considerations of Nietzsche. Some argue that Nietzsche's philosophy is dangerous, that it perhaps fed the rise of Hitler's National Socialism. It is true that Nietzsche was appropriated by the Nazis, to some extent anyway. It is also true that Nietzsche himself would have despised this: he is openly critical of nationalism, in particular German nationalism, socialism, racial purity, and anti-Semitism.

Nietzsche is in fact openly critical of almost everything, and it might be his remarkable critical power that, ultimately, makes Nietzsche both interesting and difficult. When Nietzsche is in the business of teasing out and examining cultural or moral presuppositions, he is at the height of his powers. But perhaps the occasional critical excess leaves the reader with no clear conception of Nietzsche's positive doctrine, to say nothing of arguments for his views. If, in the end, what we have in *Zarathustra* is the identification of a problem associated with value, along with a self-consistent solution, we might be forgiven for searching for other solutions. Given Nietzsche's insistence that we seek out or create value ourselves, it is hard to think that he would have scope to object.

16   The Logic of Scientific Discovery
Karl Popper (1902–94)

Popper is certainly among the twentieth century's most influential philosophers of science. It is possible to think of him as the most influential one, and certainly many argue that the explosion of interest in the philosophy of science in the last century is more or less a consequence of Popper's writings. Others, though, have little time for him. He fought his corner vigorously, they say, but not very well. Certainly he went off, late in life, in the direction of unspeakably dubious views about the objectivity of theories and the nature of the mind. We are probably too historically close to Popper to gauge his standing accurately, so we will look away from worries about his place in the history of philosophy and just attend to his views on the nature of science.

His most important book on the philosophy of science, *The Logic of Scientific Discovery*, makes two very large claims about scientific enquiry. First, Popper argues for a version of falsificationism, the view that science proceeds not by verifying the truth of hypotheses, but by putting aside false ones. Falsificationism, Popper contends, solves, or at least saves us from, the dreaded problem of induction. Second, Popper argues that scientific propositions are different from pseudo- or non-scientific propositions because they are empirically falsifiable. You can find your way into both claims by thinking, again, about Hume.

The problems of induction and demarcation

Recall that Hume noticed a problem with the justification of what he called 'causal reasoning', a difficulty in the logic of thinking our way to facts beyond the horizon of our current sensory experience. Hume argues that going beyond our current experiences requires us to think about those experiences as causes or effects of things not around at the moment. I see footprints on the beach and, knowing from past experience that such things are the effects of a person walking along before me, I conclude that someone walked along the beach before me.

This sort of reasoning seems to depend on the principle of induction, something which links many particular observations to a general conclusion. The principle gets put in a number of ways: the future will be like the past, nature is uniform, things will go along pretty much as they always have, and so on. When I conclude that a person walking was the cause of the footprints, I'm making something like the following inductive inference: 'Here are some footprints. I have seen many particular instances of footprints in the past. On each past occasion, the prints have been caused by a person walking. So, all such prints are caused by people. Therefore these footprints were caused by someone walking along the beach before me.' The principle of induction, Hume argues, underpins the inductive inference from many particular observations to a general claim – in this case, the move from encountering many footprints caused by people walking to the conclusion that all such prints are caused by people walking. It is on the basis of the general claim about all footprints that I think I know something about the cause of the footprints I happen to see.

The trouble Hume identifies, and the problem of induction for us, is that the principle of induction itself has no rational justification. Hume argues that justifiable propositions are of just two types: matters of fact and relations of ideas. We can determine whether or not an alleged matter of fact is true by having a look at the world. Relations of ideas are definitional truths or truths which get to be true in virtue of symbolic convention. Hume argues that we can spot relations of ideas because negating one results in a contradiction. As you will no doubt recall, Hume showed that the principle of induction cannot be a relation of ideas, because its negation implies no contradiction, and it cannot be justified on empirical grounds, as this would amount to arguing in a circle. There is no contradiction in thinking that the future might not be like the past after all, and you are just arguing in a circle if you say that the future will be like the past because past futures always have been like past pasts. The inductive principle, in other words, has no grounding in reason.

If you think for a moment about scientific enquiry in this connection, you can come around to the conclusion, fairly rapidly, that science itself is not rational. At first blush, science proceeds by experimentation, by racking up a number of particular observations and concluding, on the basis of them, that some general claim is true. In other words, science gets underway by noticing that several instances of a type of thing have been observed to possess a certain sort of property. Given the principle of induction, a general conclusion is reached, saying roughly that all things of that type have the property in question. This gas gets warmer when the pressure on it rises; this gas gets warmer in the same way; so too this one; therefore the temperature of all gases increases with an increase in pressure. This is induction if anything is, and if Hume is right about the irrationality of the principle of induction, science looks, at bottom, irrational. And if science is irrational, what is the difference between scientific enquiry and New Age lunacy? If you want to predict the behaviour of gases under pressure, why not consult a reader of pigeon entrails instead of a scientist?

Popper's two problems, then, concern the role of induction in science and the difference between science and pseudo-science. His solution to both involves the idea of falsification. We will take up each in turn.

Induction and falsification

Popper solves the problem of induction by replacing the inductivist conception of scientific enquiry with something else, namely falsification. Scientists need not proceed by inductively inferring general claims from many observations. Instead, the practice of science involves putting forward and then testing general theoretical claims. In other words, science does not have to infer theories from observations – this lumps us with the problem of induction. Instead scientists can deductively infer observational consequences from theories and then, on the basis of their deductions, subject the theory to rigorous testing. If testing shows that the theory predicts false observation statements, we know that the theory itself is false.

Popper's move depends on an interesting logical asymmetry. One way of thinking of the problem of induction is to notice that, no matter how many observations you might record in favour of your inductive conclusion, the conclusion might still end up false. This is just to say that inductive inferences are not logically valid. You can have entirely true premises in an inductive inference and still end up with a false conclusion. Suppose that this footprint was caused by a person walking along the beach, so was this one, and this one, and so on for as many observations as you like. My inductive conclusion that all footprints are caused by people walking along the beach can still turn out to be false, even though all my premises are true. All it takes are a few creative children making a single false footprint on a beach.

But notice what happens if we flip the logic of the situation around and think only deductively. I start with the theory that all footprints are caused by people walking along the beach. Suppose we deduce from this the observational claim that the footprints observed on Jones Beach tomorrow will be caused by people walking along the beach. We can go to the beach and have a look, and maybe all of them will be caused by people walking, but if we find just one set of false prints created by children, then we know for sure our theory is false. Induction never gets us anywhere in particular, but falsification at least can tell us when our theory is incorrect.

Popper advocates, roughly, a shift from inductive argumentation to an argument form which logicians call 'modus tollens'. Such arguments have this structure: if p entails q, and q is false, then p is false. Translated into the philosophy of science, Popper is suggesting that the rationality of science consists in the same sort of logical form: if my theory entails a particular observation, and experience contradicts that predicted observation, then my theory is false. If we cannot have inductive certainty of the truth of our theories, we can, nevertheless, sometimes have deductive certainty of their falsity. We should, therefore, reject the false ones and carry on with the ones not yet falsified.

The demarcation criterion

You can also see, again fairly quickly, how falsification informs Popper's solution to the second problem, finding a distinction between science and pseudo-science. Characterizing this distinction – setting out 'the criterion of demarcation', as Popper puts it – will go some way towards helping us to understand what science is. It will also put paid to dubious practices which sometimes get a little too much attention, particularly when they are mistaken for science. Popper was, for a time, in the service of the Freudian Alfred Adler, and thinking about Freudianism in this connection can help a little.

Suppose I bother you with my Freudian theory that the unconscious sexual desire for maternal figures underpins male behaviour. You insist on evidence, and we repair to the pub to observe customers interacting with both the man and the woman who are tending the bar. A male customer approaches the woman for a drink first, and I shout, 'Ah Ha! His unconscious desire for his mother led him to interact first with her! This proves my theory.' But if things had happened differently, and the customer approached the barman, I might just as easily have said, 'Ah Ha! He is attempting to overcome his desire for his mother by avoiding the woman behind the bar! This proves my theory.'

The trouble for Freud and to some extent Marx, by Popper's lights, is that their views are not falsifiable. A Freudian hypothesis has no empirical consequences, and that is why we should hesitate to think of it as scientific. What distinguishes science from mere pseudo-science like Freudianism is precisely the testability of scientific hypotheses. Scientific theories have consequences which we can check through observation. It is worth noting in this connection that Popper's demarcation criterion had something of an influence on the

Logical Positivists (and no doubt they had an influence on him) but his aims were certainly different. Popper never argues that claims with no empirical or observational consequences are meaningless or non-sensical. <u>Rather, his point is that science makes claims which stand a chance of conflicting with observation. Pseudo-science never does.</u>

Troubles for Popper's view

There are a number of worries associated with Popper's conception of science, despite the possibility that he gets around the problem of induction and manages to distinguish science from its pretenders. You can find your way into the difficulties by thinking about how the falsificationist view is supposed to work in practice. For example, are we to think of scientists as genuinely in the business of trying to falsify and not prove their theories? Popper seems to be saying this or something very close to it: 'I can therefore gladly admit that falsificationists like myself much prefer an attempt to solve an interesting problem by a bold conjecture, *even (and especially) if it soon turns out to be false*, to any recital of a sequence of irrelevant truisms. . . .'

Very well, a bold conjecture which turns out to be false might be preferable to irrelevancies, but are we expected to believe that scientists should be or are falsificationists? Do they jump up and down with joy when they find out the theory they have been working on, perhaps for decades, is false? Ought they to do so? You can be forgiven for thinking that Popper's efforts to dodge the problem of induction have landed him with something unlike science as it is practised or even unlike science as it ought to be practised. <u>A glance at the history of science suggests that scientists themselves do not think that they are teasing out falsehoods, but finding truth.</u> Popper's view, anyway, seems to ignore the social dimension of science as it is practised, a fact exploited by later philosophers of science such as T . S. Kuhn and Paul Feyerabend.

Thinking about the practice of science reminds us that science is supposed to have practical aims, at least some of the time. We might argue about whether science, ultimately, is in the business of improving life or, instead, if science is fundamentally a pure enquiry which aims at finding out about the world. But either view runs into trouble if you buy into Popper's conception of science. If Popper is right and we can never know whether or not a theory is true, then, rather bizarrely, science tells us nothing about the world except what is not true of it. If all we can know is that a theory is false, we end up with no positive scientific beliefs about the world.

Further, if Popper is right, in what sense can science improve life or help us make practical choices? How do we know which of our currently not-yet-falsified theories is the best guide for action? Popper's answer is a little unnerving: theories which have survived ruthless testing should guide us. Unless we fall back into induction, though, we have no reason to take this advice.

It is also true that science as it is practised does not consist in deducing observational consequences from nothing more than single theoretical claims. Even if you want to be a falsificationist, you are going to have some trouble dealing with the possibility that theories do not, by themselves, entail much of anything in the way of predictions. Additional auxiliary hypotheses are required. For example, suppose my theory says that substance-X kills germ-14. In order to test my theory, we have to bring in a whole flock of extra assumptions about the conditions for testing the presence of substance-X, the death of germ-14, not to mention further hypotheses about the microscopes we are using and the initial conditions required for our test. Suppose we do the experiment and germ-14 burbles along happily in a microscopic sea of substance-X. We might think that the theory is now falsified, but we could locate the trouble anywhere else among the auxiliary assumptions needed to deduce our prediction from the theory, and thus preserve the truth of the theory itself. Maybe our microscope was not set up quite right; perhaps we did not use enough substance-X; perhaps that was not really germ-14 in the first place; the slides might have been dirty; maybe all of the samples were corrupt; and so on for as long as you like.

Surely, you might want to say, if a theory predicts something and that prediction is contradicted by observation, then the theory is false. If your conception of planetary motion issues in the consequence that Mars will crash into us tomorrow, and it does not, then your theory is mistaken. We can quibble about the auxiliary hypotheses, but perhaps we might test each one of those too. It is observation which matters. What else could matter to scientific enquiry?

This point can be taken, but you still might wonder whether observations are as solid as the objection supposes. <u>Some argue that observation statements themselves are theory-laden. In other words, all observations depend on some theory, even very low-level theory.</u> Popper admits this, arguing that statements about observations, like theoretical statements, are themselves tentative, accepted by convention, and susceptible to testing too. He writes:

> The empirical basis of objective science has thus nothing 'absolute' about it. Science does not rest upon solid bedrock. The bold structure of its theories rises, as it were, above a swamp. It is like a building erected on piles. The piles are driven down from above into the swamp, but not down to any natural or 'given' base . . .

Does it make sense to think of theories as things which can be falsified by observation, if observation is as shaky a thing as this? Does it make any more sense to hope for something 'given' in observation? Probably we, like Popper, are bumping into a very old difficulty here, which has to do with the relation between our observations or perceptions of the world and the world itself. We might quibble with the particulars of Popper's take on the nature of science and still applaud him for showing a generation of philosophers that the philosophy of science is really a large, deep and interesting thing.

17   Language, Truth and Logic
A. J. Ayer (1910–89)

Ayer gets more than his fair share of criticism. He is considered, by many, as a brilliant but unoriginal thinker who merely brought the views of others to the English-speaking world. Whether you think the charge is warranted or not, it is hard to understand *Language, Truth and Logic* without knowing at least a little about the Vienna Circle and Logical Positivism. We will consider both, then take up Ayer's book in some detail.

The Vienna Circle

The Vienna Circle was a group of scientifically minded philosophers and philosophically minded scientists. The group's membership shifted but at one time or another it included Otto Neurath, Rudolph Carnap, Philip Frank, Moritz Schlick, Herbert Feigl and Kurt Gödel. They met informally in the decades before the Second World War to discuss a range of issues, particularly those having to do with meaning in both philosophy and science. All had an interest in logic and language, and their influences read like a 'Who's Who of Analytic Philosophy'. This makes considerable sense, since the Circle and the thinkers they studied more or less hammered out the foundation of analytic philosophy as it is practised today. Wittgenstein's *Tractatus* was read line by line – of particular importance to the Circle were his views on the nature of meaning and the formal structure of a logical language. Popper's thoughts on the distinction between science, which deals with testable hypotheses, and pseudo-science, which does not, also had a large influence. Tarski's work on formal semantics was taken on board. Frege, Russell and Whitehead were concerned with high-powered conceptions of logic and mathematics, and the Circle took to their work with relish. You can form the idea from all of this, no doubt rightly, that the Vienna Circle was tough-minded. They took science as the paradigm of rationality and generally disdained the wishy-washy claims of metaphysics, religion and to some extent ethics and aesthetics.

They became synonymous with Logical Positivism, one of the largest philosophical movements of the twentieth century. Logical Positivism is generally understood as rooted in a thesis about a criterion of meaning, the so-called 'verification principle'. The meaning of a sentence, according to the view, is given by specifying the steps which might be taken to verify its truth or falsity. Knowing the meaning of 'Sulphur is yellow when burned' amounts to knowing that burning some sulphur and having a look at the colour of the flame will tell you whether or not the sentence is true. What is most important for Logical Positivism is not the truth or falsity of sentences – working out that sort of thing is the job of the natural sciences – but the meaning of sentences. The sentence 'Sulphur is yellow when burned' has meaning because we know what to do to find out whether or not it is true; we know what observations would count towards determining its truth or falsity. The sentence has meaning because it has empirical content; observations matter to its truth value; it says something precisely because it says something about the world.

Think for a moment about what might happen if the verification principle is applied to talk about metaphysics, religion, morality and aesthetics. Consider this passage from Heidegger's *Being and Time*:

> Temporality temporalizes itself fully in each ecstasy, i.e. in the ecstatic unity of the complete temporalizing of temporality there is grounded the wholeness of the structural complex of existentiality, factuality and fallenness, which comprises the unity of the care-structure.

Well, do you have any idea at all how this sentence might be verified? What observations could possibly tell you whether or not it is true? If you are drawing a blank and are persuaded that the verification principle is the right way to think about meaning, then you have to conclude that the sentence is literally nonsense. It is not only Heidegger, but also whole classes of philosophical claims – 'the soul is immortal'; 'the universe is one'; 'murder is wrong'; 'the beautiful is sublime' – that make no sense from the Logical Positivist point of view.

Ayer sat in on the discussions of the Vienna Circle in 1932 and 1933, returned to Oxford, and completed *Language, Truth and Logic* by 1935. Weighing in at just over 150 pages, it is a pipsqueak when compared to the extravagant lengths of some philosophical master-pieces, but a heavyweight contender in terms of content. In it, Ayer says that he has dispensed with metaphysics; offered an account of the nature of meaning, truth and probability; formulated a theory of ethical discourse; proven theism nonsensical; solved the problem of induction; dealt with questions about the self and the external world; and provided philosophy with a clear conception of its point and purpose. He sorts out the problem of free will in a footnote. The book is gutsy, crisp, clear and concise, which is a large part of its enduring attraction. Published when he was just 24, it is, as Ayer puts it, 'a young man's book . . . written with more passion than most philosophers allow themselves to show'. The arguments for his bold conclusions hang on his version of the verification principle.

The verification principle

Ayer joins the long tradition of empiricists who recognize a distinc-tion between two sorts of genuine proposition. Following Hume, Ayer splits all genuine propositions into two classes: what Hume called 'relations of ideas' and 'matters of fact'. The former include the *a priori* truths of mathematics and logic; such propositions do not say anything about how the world is, but express the ways in which we use certain symbols. Everything left over may or may not be a matter of fact. Genuine matters of fact are hypotheses, statements of how the world is or might be, which stand a chance of being either true of false. The remainder are pseudo-propositions, statements which do not say anything which might be true or false and are, therefore, without cognitive meaning. The verification principle tells us the difference between empirical propositions and pseudo-propositions. Ayer writes: 'We say that a sentence is factually significant to any given person, if, and only if, he knows how to verify the proposition which it purports to express – that is, if he knows what observations would lead him, under certain conditions, to accept the proposition as being true, or reject it as being false.'

Ayer's version of the verification principle departs in a number of ways from the thinking of some of the members of the Vienna Circle. First of all, Ayer distinguishes between practical verifiability and verifiability in principle. If you leave the verification principle as is, you are left wondering about the extent to which we might know what observations would lead us to accept scientific propositions which we do not have the means to verify at present. To borrow Ayer's example, at the time of the writing of *Language, Truth and Logic*, the right sort of rockets had not yet been invented, so no one could check on the truth of the proposition expressed by the sentence, 'The far side of the moon is mountainous.' But even without the technology, you could still know what observations would decide the truth of the claim – the observations are theoretically conceivable, even if no one as yet knows how to get a pair of eyeballs into position to make the relevant observations. The proposition is, therefore, verifiable in principle but not in practice. Verifiability in principle is enough for us to say that the proposition has meaning, according to Ayer.

A second distinction between strong and weak verification is also required. The strong sense of 'verification' holds that a proposition is verifiable if and only if its truth could be conclusively established by observation; the weak sense of 'verification' holds that a proposition is verifiable if and only if it is possible for experience to render it probable. You might wonder whether propositions about the past or the future or, worse for Logical Positivism, the general statements which make up a good part of theoretical science are themselves verifiable. What observation or set of observations could lead you to accept that 'Millard Fillmore was the thirteenth president of the United States' or 'Metals tend to expand when heated' or even 'All men are mortal'? You have less of a problem if you opt for weak verification and maintain that observation need not conclusively establish the truth or falsity of a proposition. This Ayer does.

Analysis

We have already seen the effects of the verification principle on metaphysics, and you might wonder, with metaphysics gone, whether philosophy has any function left to serve. Ayer argues that philosophy just cannot be in the business of deducing a picture of reality from first principles, as perhaps many of the great philosophers might have thought. There can be no first principles of the required sort: we cannot 'advance a single step' beyond what is immediately given in experience by mere deduction; *a priori* principles are tautologies, and only more tautologies can be deduced from them. Philosophy, instead, is in the business of clarification and analysis.

Philosophy does not enquire into the nature of the world or even describe it: philosophy is the analysis of language. It expresses definitions and the logical consequences of definitions. Philosophy, for Ayer, 'is a department of logic'. The practice is not concerned with explicit definition, that is to say, defining a word with synonyms. Instead it ferrets out definitions in use which, for Ayer, are translations of symbols which do not contain either the symbol or synonyms of the symbol.

Consider his treatment of perception. Talking about material objects, for Ayer, is analysed in terms of talk about sense-contents, which you might think of as the sensory items directly experienced in a perceptual event. He says that two sense-contents directly resemble one another when there is no or only a little difference in quality between them. Two sense-contents indirectly resemble one another when they are tied together by a series of direct resemblances. Two visual experiences are directly continuous when they belong to a series of sense experiences with no discernible qualitative differences among the members of the series. Two visual experiences are indirectly continuous when they are related by a series of direct continuities. So, for any two sense-contents, Ayer says that they are elements of the same material thing if and only if 'they are related to one another by a relation of direct, or indirect, resemblance in certain respects and by a relation of direct, or indirect, continuity'. The analysis goes into further detail, but you can see just from this snippet that Ayer sees philosophy as working through definitions of a certain sort, and with them coming to truth through the analysis of language.

Emotivism

Perhaps the most infamous part of the book is Ayer's treatment of ethics. His general thesis in this neighbourhood is that statements of value are either really only ordinary scientific statements, in which case they have meaning, or they are not scientific, in which case they are merely expressions of emotion and as such are neither true nor false. He divides the activities of past ethical philosophers into four classes. The first group, defining ethical terms, is genuine moral philosophy. The second group, formulating descriptions of moral experience and its causes, is properly the business of the science of psychology or sociology. The third group, making exhortations in favour of moral virtue, contains no meaningful propositions at all. The fourth group, engaging in actual ethical judgements, cannot be a part of moral philosophy – philosophy itself is analysis, not the making of individual moral judgements.

When Ayer attempts genuine moral philosophy – for him the analysis of ethical terms – he ends up with the view that ethical concepts are not analysable, because there is no objective criterion by means of which one might determine the validity of such judgements. That is to say, for Ayer, that ethical concepts fail the criterion for meaning set out by the verification principle. Ethical concepts are pseudo-concepts, concepts which add nothing to the factual content of propositions. The sentence 'You acted wrongly in stealing that money' adds no further facts than those indicated by the sentence

'You stole that money'. What gets added by moral concepts, if anything, is nothing more than the expression of approval or disapproval for some actions and not others.

Generalizing from the particular case above, Ayer argues that if I say 'Stealing money is wrong', I produce a sentence which has no factual meaning; it expresses no proposition which can be either true or false. 'It is as if I had written "Stealing money!!" – where the shape and thickness of the exclamation marks shows, by a suitable convention, that a special sort of moral disapproval is the feeling which is being expressed.' It follows from this that there is no fact of the matter concerning the moral part of moral disagreements. If you claim that stealing money is wrong, and I insist that stealing money is right, what we are doing is expressing different emotions towards a kind of action.

For Ayer, there is no sense in asking which one of us is right about stealing money. No genuine propositions are being asserted by either one of us – no one is stating a fact so there are no facts to dispute. Moral disagreements, insofar as they are moral, are not really factual disagreements at all. We can dispute the facts of a given case – argue about the motive of the thief or her special circumstances – but when we fall into the morality of the question at hand, we become nothing more than cheerleaders for our particular moral viewpoint.

Ayer took rather a lot of heat for his version of the emotive theory of ethical discourse – the so-called 'Boo! Hurrah!' theory. Many argued that it simply missed out what is fundamental to morality, which is more than just the expression of sentiment. Emotivism has a hard time dealing with what we should do not when we dispute with others about moral questions, but when we face a moral dilemma ourselves and try to think our way through it.

Objections to Ayer

The strongest objections to Ayer, though, come from reflection on the verification principle itself. The largest problem, considered by

Ayer among several others in the Preface to the 1946 edition of the book, has to do with the general difficulty the principle has with ruling out metaphysically excessive propositions and retaining scientific ones.

Recall that Ayer was led to opt for weak verification in order to keep certain scientific propositions. His reason for doing so concerns the fact that science sometimes proceeds by showing that a statement about a particular observation is deducible from a scientific proposition in conjunction with other, auxiliary propositions. It turns out that any proposition at all – even something egregiously metaphysical like 'the Absolute is lazy' – can be rendered meaningful according to the verification principle by tying it to certain auxiliary propositions and observation statements. You can plug in not just the scientific claims Ayer wants to preserve, but any claim at all, and Ayer is stuck with the view that whatever claim you insert counts as meaningful. Ayer tried to correct the problem in the new preface, but logicians quickly showed that even his amendments were no help. The verification principle is far too liberal.

Other critics, perhaps with a little too much glee, point out that if the principle could be ironed out and saved from charges of excessive liberalism, it would nevertheless render itself meaningless. What observations would lead one to accept the following proposition as being true or reject it as being false: 'A sentence is factually significant to any given person, if, and only if, he knows how to verify the proposition which it purports to express – that is, if he knows what observations would lead him, under certain conditions, to accept the proposition as being true, or reject it as being false'? Well, no observation fits the bill, so the principle seems to self-destruct.

Ayer's response to the claim that the verification principle is self-defeating is, in part, to say that the principle itself is not the sort of proposition to which the principle applies. It is an expression of a definition or analysis of meaning. Such a definition can, of course, be matched by formulating a different definition of meaning which keeps metaphysics, religion and the rest. There is nothing to choose between the definitions, so why pick Ayer's version?

Philosophy has largely moved on from both Logical Positivism and the verification principle, but analysis is still very much with us, and so is the philosophy of Ayer. He is still required reading in epistemology and metaphysics, and his treatment of value still has vocal adherents. We have kept the practice of analysis if not the version of the practice espoused by Ayer and the Vienna Circle. In fact, in most of the USA and Great Britain, the practice just *is* philosophy.

18   Being and Nothingness
Jean-Paul Sartre (1905–80)

Jean-Paul Sartre stands in the grand French tradition of polymath writers. He was a novelist, playwright, journalist, biographer, literary critic and polemicist, as well as a philosopher. *Being and Nothingness* presents a sophisticated and nuanced theory of the nature of human beings, their place in the world, and their understanding of them-selves and one another. Although Sartre was already known as a writer in France, chiefly for his classic philosophical novel *Nausea*, it was this treatise and the popularizations of its central themes in his novels and plays of the mid-1940s that catapulted him to the centre of French intellectual life, where he remained until his death in 1980. Within a couple of years of publication, the term 'existentialism' had been invented to summarize his philosophy, though Sartre soon muddied the waters by extending the term to various of his heroes despite their fundamental disagreements with his philosophy, not to mention their disagreements with one another. This seems to have licensed the subsequent extension of the term to all manner of writers, artists, playwrights and film-makers whose works were only partly related to Sartre's philosophy.

The book itself is stylistically a little schizophrenic. Many passages exhibit a kind of lucidity, owing partly to the finely honed descrip-tive skills of Sartre as successful novelist and playwright. Such pas-sages usually centre on his trademark accounts of the comical yet familiar behaviour of various characters, their foibles and reactions as much as their deliberate actions. Other passages, on the other hand, are dense and difficult, and they require some deciphering. These are generally concerned with his ambitious attempt to for-mulate, express and defend an obscure metaphysical view in dia-logue with some of his more abstruse predecessors. Sartre is fast and loose in his discussions of other philosophers, having little time for careful scholarship or possible responses to his criticisms, which has led some to consider the work confused and populist, lacking in the academic rigour required of philosophy. Such dismissals, though, are probably too quick. The massive impact that the book had on twentieth-century intellectual culture is due to its acute, penetrating and often disconcerting insights into our everyday engagement with the world and with one another, and these insights deserve our attention.

Being and Nothingness

The metaphysical grounding for Sartre's insights lies, as the book's title suggests, in the relation between being and its opposite, the absence of being, which he calls 'non-being' or 'nothingness'. This use of the term 'being' is grammatically unwieldy, but his basic idea is that something can have being (or, better, something can *be*) in either of two ways. Tables and chairs, oceans and trees, pebbles and planets, are all made of a substance that has being-in-itself (or, which *is* in itself). That is to say that they just are: they do not depend on our awareness of them, or on God or anything similar, and they just are what they are. An individual person, on the other hand, has being-for-itself (or, *is* for itself). People are aware of their surroundings, but more crucially they are aware of themselves, and they have aims they want to achieve and projects to pursue. Someone might be a student today, aiming to be a lawyer in the future. An oak tree is kind of stuck: it cannot aim or even wish to be an elm tree, or indeed anything else. What distinguishes us from material objects is chiefly this concern with our own place in the world.

The world as we experience it is not just made up of these two types of beings. The world also contains nothingness. While this may sound strange, the example Sartre uses to support it is perfectly mundane. If I arrange to meet my friend Pierre at a certain café, I arrive 15 minutes late, and I know that Pierre is always punctual, then when I enter the café and see that he is not there, his absence stands out against the background of the café. What I experience, what I *see* in the café, is the *absence* of Pierre. Sartre insists that this absence is experienced, rather than simply something I can judge on the basis of the stuff that I experience. It is not that I look around the room, notice all the things that are there, and then conclude via a process of thought that Pierre is not among them. I could do that, of course, but the experience of noticing that he is not there is not like this. His absence is not like the absence of, say, Napoleon or Socrates from the café. These I can judge, but Pierre's absence strikes me in the same way as his presence would, were he there. As Sartre puts it, 'my expectation has caused the absence of Pierre to *happen* as a real event concerning this café'.

This is one example of what Sartre calls the 'little pools of non-being' that we notice around us in everyday life. Other examples he gives range from finding that, yet again, I do not have enough money in my wallet, to missing a loved one who is away or deceased. These are examples of nothingness, or non-being, because what is experienced is not a thing but the absence of a thing, so what is noticed is part of the experienced world only because of the expectations or desires of the person who experiences it. It has no being in itself. But these are not the only kinds of nothingness in the world.

In addition to the nothingnesses we find alongside the beings we encounter, there are the nothingnesses that pervade all of those beings. This kind of nothingness is 'that by which the world receives its outlines as a world'. When we encounter an object as an individual object, then we encounter it as other than its surroundings: the chair stands out as *not being* one with the desk or the floor. The individuation of objects in experience therefore involves nothingness. Our experience of the world is also pervaded with instrumental, moral and aesthetic values: the chair is experienced as something for sitting on, violence is experienced as abhorrent, art is experienced as beautiful. These evaluative aspects of our experience reflect our purposes in the world; they are not simply things which exist independently of us: 'in this world where I engage myself, my acts cause values to spring up like partridges'. Since these values have no being in themselves, they are nothingnesses.

Freedom

It is on the basis of this account of the relation between mind and world that Sartre builds his theories of the freedom of the individual, and his related theories of 'bad faith' and 'the look'. The actions a person performs are motivated by the way the world seems to that person but, since this is already dependent on her purposes in the world, we cannot say that individuals simply respond to the way being in itself is arranged. The reason I tidied my room is not simply that the papers and books were strewn across the floor, but that the room looked untidy and hence unsatisfactory to me, and it looked this way because of the kind of life I lead or maybe should lead. While the unsatisfactory untidiness of the room might seem like a fact about the room, this is because it is an aspect of how I see the room; 'the man who is angry sees on the face of his opponent the objective quality of asking for a punch on the nose'. It is not just that our action depends on the kinds of lives we lead in this way, but the lives we lead cannot be motivated purely by the nature of our material surroundings either. Instead, these reflect choices we have made about how to respond to the condition of being material beings in a material world.

This part of *Being and Nothingness* is more than a little obscure, but the basic idea seems to be that each person has the deeply held objective of identifying with a certain kind of person – whether it be a studious intellectual, a tortured genius, a resigned loser, or whatever – and this project sets limits on the other kinds of projects one will pursue. Sartre is keen to stress that we are not determined by these projects to behave in certain ways, but only to be inclined to behave in those ways. We can, he thinks, resist these inclinations, behave in ways contrary to them, and in this way break free of the projects we otherwise pursue. Not only were our projects chosen in the dim and distant past, they are also constantly reaffirmed as we go about our daily business, unless we overthrow them in favour of new projects.

This theory of freedom is encapsulated in the apparently contradictory formula known as 'Sartre's paradox': where a being-in-itself simply 'is what it is', a being-for-itself 'is a being which is what it is not and which is not what it is'. You might want to read that again. The point is that you are what you are not, for Sartre, in the sense that in order to define you in such a way that we can understand your behaviour, we need that definition to make reference to the projects you are pursuing and hence the kind of person you wish to be identified with or to become, which is something that you are not or are not yet. To say that you are not what you are is to say that even when we have given this definition, your behaviour is not determined by all the facts that it refers to: you may still resist the inclinations that are rooted in your projects and behave in new and entirely unpredictable ways.

We have some awareness of this freedom, Sartre thinks, but prefer to brush it under the carpet. Walking along a cliff-top path, you might suddenly realize that there is nothing whatsoever preventing you from throwing yourself over the side. You could simply jump off the cliff. This does not mean that you are motivated to do so, of course, but Sartre is interested in precisely this realization that you *could* jump despite having no reason to. This realization he terms 'anguish in the face of the future'. There is also the related 'anguish in the face of the past', epitomized by the person who has resolved never to gamble again being tempted by the thought of a visit to the casino. However sincere our resolutions, they must be remade at every moment if we are to keep them. Our actions are not fully determined by our resolutions, our aims or our projects. In calling this awareness of our freedom 'anguish', Sartre refers to our awareness of the terrible sense of responsibility that comes with it. If my actions are really under my control in this way and to this extent, then there is nothing at all I can blame for any action I would rather not have committed. Neither heredity nor upbringing nor traumatic past events determine my current behaviour. I am without excuse.

There is a liberationist tenor to much of *Being and Nothingness*, despite Sartre's insistence that the book makes no ethical or political pronouncements. This tone is most prominent in his discussion of bad faith, and most obvious in his use of that epithet. We attempt to evade anguish, to deny our freedom and its attendant responsibility, through various strategies. Sartre's most famous example is his caricature of a

Parisian waiter, whose movement is 'a little too precise, a little too rapid', who tries 'to imitate in his walk the inflexible stiffness of some kind of automaton' and carries his tray 'with the recklessness of a tightrope walker by putting it in a perpetually unstable, perpetually broken equilibrium which he perpetually re-establishes by a light movement of the arm and hand'. This waiter, Sartre claims, is trying to convince himself and his customers that he is a waiter in the same way as a coffee pot is a coffee pot. He is attempting, that is, to deny his freedom and hence his responsibility for his actions by acting as though he has a fixed nature that determines all his behaviour, just as a chunk of being-in-itself has a fixed nature. The waiter here is meant simply as a representative. Sartre gives a host of other examples, and implies that most people approach life in this way. Though he hardly ever mentions it, he does seem to think that we can and should escape this bad faith and take up instead an attitude of 'authenticity', in which we affirm the true nature of our being.

Other people

It is not just our own being that we approach in this way. We also misunderstand one another in exactly the same way. Motivated by jealousy, you might be looking through a keyhole to see what is going on in another room when you hear footsteps in the hall behind you and are suddenly overcome with shame. This emotion belies the belief that the other person categorizes you in some undesirable way, perhaps as a voyeur or a snoop. You are taking the other person as seeing you as having some property that determines your behaviour in the way in which the properties of material objects determine their behaviour, and this property is an undesirable one. Sartre calls this 'the look'.

Our response to it is simply to categorize the other person in ways that undermine their categorization of us. We consider them judgemental, puritanical, stupid, or whatever, and we consider this property to have determined their categorization of us. Sartre does not think that this scenario occurs only on particular kinds of occasion, but rather that we enter into these relations of mutual categorization all the time. The conflict that this engenders is, he says, the basis of social relations. As his character Garcin famously puts it in the play variously translated as *In Camera* and *No Exit*, 'Hell is other people'.

Commentators disagree over exactly how to understand this. Some take Sartre to be claiming that this categorization is an inevitable aspect of our awareness of other people, part of the structure of the mind. But others take him to have the less pessimistic view that it is simply a product of bad faith: once we learn to accept what a human being truly is, we will no longer think of one another in these alienating and frustrating ways. This reading reflects the liberationist tenor of the work, Sartre's implication that we would be better off fully acknowledging something that we are in some sense already aware of: that our behaviour results ultimately from our freely chosen and revisable projects. Towards the end of the book, he sketches a method of 'existential psychoanalysis', designed to help each of us to understand the projects we have chosen, and their manifestation in our behaviour. Unlike Freudian psychoanalysis, this is not aimed at uncovering unconscious aspects of the mind (which Sartre thinks cannot exist) but at making clear and explicit something of which we are dimly and vaguely conscious. This would help us to change those aspects of our behaviour that trouble us, perhaps including the conflicting nature of our social relations.

As his thought progressed over the decades following the publication of *Being and Nothingness*, Sartre became more interested in the impact that upbringing and social status have on the projects people pursue, and his writings took on more ideas from Freud, Marx and their followers. Many commentators have understood this as a move away from the central idea of existentialism – perhaps our behaviour can only be explained in terms of the projects we freely choose to pursue. Yet Sartre claimed towards the end of his life that he had never abandoned existentialism. Perhaps these later works are better read as developments of *Being and Nothingness*, as investigating in further detail the motivations people may have for freely choosing the projects that determine their lives and destinies.

19   The Second Sex
Simone de Beauvoir (1908–86)

There are not many women in most accounts of the history of philosophy. This is not to say that there have been no women philosophers, but it is true, nevertheless, that women get left out of the story.
Some argue that this has something to do with how philosophy itself
is perceived, others say that it has more to do with how women are
perceived, still others point to social and economic factors which
push women away from philosophy or at least remove them from our
thinking about philosophy. More reasons are possible. Whatever the
reason or reasons, ignoring women in a consideration of philosophy
is an obvious error. If we can avoid this error, there are two other sorts
of mistake in this connection, and it is not easy to side-step them. You
can make mistakes in understanding a woman philosopher's work by
thinking of her as a woman philosopher, as opposed to a philosopher.
You can also make mistakes in understanding a woman philosopher's
work by ignoring the fact that she is a woman. We will do the best we
can in what follows.

De Beauvoir is known outside of philosophy as an excellent novelist and lifelong companion of Sartre, whom she cites as a large
philosophical influence. It is becoming clear that she had about as
much of an impact on his philosophy as he had on hers, but she is a
little more generous in mentioning the connection than he is. She is
also known by some as a feminist philosopher. *The Second Sex* is at
least an existentialist treatment of the nature of women, and also a
feminist or proto-feminist one. De Beauvoir, at times, did not much
like being thought of as an existentialist. Feminists, at times, do not
much like thinking of de Beauvoir as a feminist.

The book has had a strange history, in part because not many people
knew what to do with it when it was first published. It is possible that
the book had to be written before other books like it could be understood, and that situation left *The Second Sex* in a kind of limbo. The
first lines of the translator's preface to at least one edition might be

illustrative of the fact that even those ready for de Beauvoir were not exactly ready for her: 'A serious, all inclusive, and uninhibited work on a woman by a woman of wit and learning! What, I had often thought, could be more desirable and yet less to be expected?' It was received badly by some critics on its publication, but many take it that the shift in thinking about women in the 1960s was partly owed to the book. By the 1970s, at least as many feminists thought it out of date or somehow reactionary or provincial, particularly in its claim that women might find liberation by adopting what looks like a masculine self-conception. The book has recently enjoyed a resurgence, with some arguing that, because it was simultaneously influential and ignored, discovering it and reading it again makes it somehow feel postmodern, as though it has just emerged. It will take a while, probably, to understand its true place in the history of philosophy.

The work is divided into two books. The first book considers historical conceptions of women, from the point of view of biology, as well as Freudian treatments of women, the history of the place of women, and the mythology of women in poetry and literature. The second book considers the various roles of contemporary women, culminating in a consideration of the possibility of liberation and independence.

Throughout the book, de Beauvoir is dealing with the question, 'What is a woman?' The question gets a certain gloss, and it might be put this way too: 'Why is woman the other?' She begins by noting that the fact that the question is asked at all suggests something about the answer. It would never occur to a man to ask what a man is or even contemplate a book on it. Men are subjects, a kind of default conception of humanity. Women, if anything, are thought to be something else, something even less than or different from an object for the male subject. But in thinking along these Hegelian lines, which we will consider more carefully in a moment, de Beauvoir is trying to get round the usual well-worn considerations of women in particular and their secondary status. She is after a new, clear conception of women, in an effort to throw light on the following questions: 'How can a human being in a woman's situation attain fulfilment? What roads are open to her? Which are blocked? How can independence be recovered in a state of dependency? What circumstances limit a woman's liberty and how can they be overcome?'

The destiny of women

The first part of the book attempts to show that that the destiny of women is not fixed by biology, psychology or economics, or even much illuminated by these things. In other words, there is some hope for liberty. Biology is important in an attempt to answer her questions, thinks de Beauvoir, because our bodies are 'the instrument of our grasp on the world'. The sort of body you have dictates a part of your connection to things, but certainly it does not dictate everything. Her treatment of biology works through a number of examples of primarily the reproductive strategies of various insects and animals. She also considers what she takes to be simply brute biological differences between men and women. Part of her conclusion is that the human female is perhaps the most enslaved of all the mammalian females to reproduction, and also human females are the ones who most resist this. Her point in the end, though, is that biology cannot explain the hierarchy of human sexuality, why woman is thought of as the other, nor can biology keep women in their subordinate role.

If biology does not make women the other, de Beauvoir argues, we should look to conceptual history to see what humanity has made of the human female. She starts with psychoanalysis, perhaps hoping for some advance on the biological point of view, given the psychoanalytical precept that it is not nature which defines woman, but possibly she who defines herself through her emotional life. De Beauvoir makes less sport of Freud than you might expect, and even cites him authoritatively elsewhere, but notes at least for clarity's sake the troubles associated with thinking of women as merely castrated men. In the end, she argues that Freud is no help. He takes it that men are somehow dominant or at least what we think of as subject – perhaps this fact has something to do with the sovereignty of the father – but Freud starts here, without a clue as to the origin of male supremacy.

If we are after some conception of woman as a human being looking for value, then we must approach the world of value itself, and this, for de Beauvoir, has something to do with social and economic structures. De Beauvoir's talk of woman as object to man's subject is clearly informed by Hegelian thinking, and so is her view that women generally are not defined merely by the bodies or minds they have, but by their historical moment, their place given the point in social, economic and technological evolution that the species itself has attained.

She works through human history itself, Hegel-style, from reflection on nomadic people, through Antiquity, the Middle Ages and beyond the French Revolution, tracing the effects of social forces on the role and place of women in society. Her conclusion is that, despite social improvements, women are still subjugated by men – a woman 'still sees herself and makes her choices not in accordance with her true nature in itself, but as man defines her'. A woman still is, for the most part, as men 'have fancied her in their dreams'; de Beauvoir moves on to consider how it is that men have defined women in mythology and literature.

De Beauvoir's treatment of women in myth and literature is a kind of *tour de force*, and it is evident that the author has a novelist's eye. Hegel is lurking here too, as again the notion that women are other is explored, this time as a feature built into the myth-making of cultures. Creation myths, Greek and Roman mythology, Shakespeare and finally the writings of several other authors are mined for this truth, and de Beauvoir does not have to dig very deeply. The implications are brought into view. 'Few myths have been more advantageous to the ruling caste than the myth of women,' de Beauvoir bristles, 'it justifies all privileges and even authorizes their abuse'.

Absolute other

With the first book now on the table, we can pause for a moment over the role of Hegel's thinking in all of this. It is Hegel's view that the subject, to be a subject, requires another, needs to see himself as subject in the eye of another subject. In doing this, the second subject becomes a kind of object for the first. But as de Beauvoir shows in considerations of body, social standing, and mythmaking and literature, women somehow stand outside of the usual Hegelian dialectic. Because women's bodies are weaker, their standing is lesser; because social conventions are built on this, in part, women are stuck as social subordinates; and because they are mythologized differently, women are considered as something other than subjects. All of this puts women outside of the usual Hegelian subject–object dialectic. Women are other, but not the sort of other that renders the male subject a subject; men are needed for that. Women are absolute others, objects which never become subjects in the eyes of men.

The second book opens with a short statement of what might be de Beauvoir's largest point: 'One is not born, but rather becomes, a woman'. The argument of the first book leads to just this conclusion. Biology, psychology, society and the rest do not, individually, make woman what she is: 'it is civilization as a whole which produces this creature'. The point itself, and the discussion in the second book, is rooted in existentialism. The existentialist precept that essence does not precede existence is part of the warp and weft of de Beauvoir's thinking here. The view is, roughly, that human beings have no predetermined essence, and what they are is determined by how they exist, what choices they make, how they in fact act in the world.

Part of the point is that although human beings have no determinant nature, women have been defined by men as having precisely this, and the nature attached to women by others is itself part of the subjugation of women. Further, women have attempted to satisfy something like a desire for fulfilment by seeking fulfilment in men, rather than in their own projects, and this, for de Beauvoir, is a kind of inauthenticity. The trouble, then, comes from two directions. Women have their natures determined for them, by men, and women themselves fail to make the sorts of choices which might lead to authentic existence.

The experiences of women

The second book, then, traces the sorts of existences women experience: girlhood, wife, mother, as well as those who choose 'forbidden ways': lesbians and prostitutes, and finally, for all: maturity and old age. Obviously, not all roles are occupied by all women, but her discussions of childhood, being a young girl, and to some extent sexual initiation, seem intended to say something about the general sorts of experiences all or most women have which shape the sense in which they become absolute other. For example, de Beauvoir argues that a young girl cannot become a grown-up without accepting and displaying her 'femininity'. Aspects of the road to womanhood bury individuality, desires, self-expression, rebellion, independence and result, finally, in a kind of submission which is the fundamental part of womanhood as it is.

De Beauvoir turns finally to the independent woman and it is here, perhaps, that many take exception to her recommendations. She seems to advocate for women what she elsewhere condemns in men, namely an insistence on the sort of subjectivity men have achieved for women themselves. Women breaking free from men, as some read her, amounts to women taking on the properties and powers which men exhibit, doing what men do. What is needed, some argue, is not that women should become like men, but that human beings generally should change the nature of the male-dominated world in such a way that women are free to be women, not merely women who act as men do. What is wrong, by many lights, is androcentricity, and the solution is not to see authenticity as masculine life, but as cashed out by individual human lives, whatever their gender.

Hegel, Sartre and de Beauvoir

There are other troubles, too, which are not as easily identified. As we have seen, de Beauvoir's analysis of women blends Hegel and existentialism and, although the mix works for some purposes, there are some underlying tensions. The very notion of authenticity is not historical at all, and at least some of the Hegelianism in de Beauvoir's thinking is necessarily historical. Authenticity depends on people as such, beings who live lives in understanding, who choose their own identity. Hegelian dialectical materialism has it that people are who they are given their moment in history. De Beauvoir's conception of woman is informed by both Hegel and existentialism, and it is not clear that her analysis avoids the contradictions inherent in what look like opposing philosophical points of view.

De Beauvoir's thinking moved on after the publication of *The Second Sex*. She denied being a feminist until late in life, and she also rethought some of the premises contained in the book. She certainly noticed that there is a tension between the existentialist view of freedom and the kind of overwhelming oppression outlined in the book. Existentialism, on some readings, has it that there is a large sense in which the subjugation of women is largely the fault of women, a failure on the part of women to realize their own freedom. Given the book's long and compelling considerations of the many factors which shape the lives of women, it is hard to see how the radical freedom of a full-blown existentialism is possible for women. It might have shaken her faith in at least a part of existentialism, and certainly she parted company from at least some of Sartre's claims. She also added to existentialism the notion of concrete or actual possibilities, and the doctrine is the richer for it.

The book notices a lot about male–female relationships, and the vast majority of it is not at all flattering to the male. It is, or can be, surprising to notice that the book ends with a kind of call for an elevated reconciliation, which is usually missed by those who, in moments of simple-mindedness, denounce the book as simple-minded man-bashing. De Beauvoir writes: 'To gain the supreme victory, it is necessary, for one thing, that by and through their natural differentiation, men and women unequivocally affirm their brotherhood.'

20 Philosophical Investigations
Ludwig Wittgenstein (1889–1951)

Wittgenstein is certainly among the twentieth century's greatest philosophers. He made substantial contributions to the philosophy of language, logic, epistemology, the philosophy of mind and mathematics, but probably most of all, he changed the way many of us think about and practise philosophy. He brought originality to more or less every philosophical topic he touched, and the responses to his work seem to range from incomprehension to the recognition of nothing less than a philosophical revolution. We are, it seems, still trying to decide what to do with him.

His first book, *Tractatus Logico-Philosophicus*, is about as odd as the conditions of its writing warrant. Wittgenstein wrote it while serving in the Austrian army during the First World War. It consists of seven numbered propositions, all but the last followed by further explanatory comments. The relative importance of and explanatory connections between the comments are indicated by decimal numbers. So, for example, he writes: '1 The world is all that is the case', which is followed by '1.1 The world is the totality of facts, not of things', which is followed by '1.11 The world is determined by the facts, and by their being *all* the facts.' Proposition (1) is the main claim, elucidated by proposition (1.1), which itself is followed by (1.11), a commentary on (1.1). You can probably tell by just these few examples that the propositions which constitute the *Tractatus* are sometimes more than a little gnomic. The book is only about 75 pages long, but it can take quite a while to read. You have to put it down and stare out of a window at regular intervals to find your way through it.

The views elucidated in the *Tractatus*, for all its pithy brevity, were eventually and comprehensively rejected by Wittgenstein. In particular, the book's central claim that the meaning of a word is what the word stands for was seen as a mistake, an error he came to recognize and correct during 16 years of teaching and reflection at Cambridge.

His new view started to circulate among students and colleagues in the form of two unpublished sets of lecture notes dictated to his students from 1933–5. The first was bound in blue wrappers and the second in brown wrappers – they came to be known as 'the Blue and the Brown Books'. Students and friends made their own copies and passed them around. He thought about revising and publishing them, but eventually inscribed this in a margin: 'This whole attempt at a revision, from the start right up to this point, is *worthless*.'

The lecture notes were still in circulation, though, and the thought that they might turn into his legacy, he says, 'stung my vanity'. He thought they were watered-down and generally not expressive of his new conception of language. He began preparing *Philosophical Investigations*, which remained unfinished at his death. Whereas the *Tractatus* is a kind of monument to organization, a regimented march of numbered sentences appearing in a precise order, *Philosophical Investigations* is a calm and meandering stroll across a countryside. Or, as he puts it, the book is a series of poorly executed sketches of a landscape, seen from different points of view, which come together in a kind of album. There are no chapter headings – no chapters for that matter – and there is no introduction or conclusion. The book really is a series of remarks – part of the way Wittgenstein thinks philosophy has to be done – a collection of investigations coming at the same questions or topics from several directions. We will examine some of it.

Conceptions of language

First, it will help to contrast his new view of language with the earlier version set forth in the *Tractatus*. In the latter, he argues for the picture theory of meaning, the view that propositions are logical pictures or models of states of affairs in the world. Just as a visual picture or a three-dimensional model can depict a person, a sentence is a logical picture of part of the world. The meanings of words are the things those words stand for or signify. If a proposition gets it right, not only do the words match up to the things they stand for, but the formal or logical structure of the proposition also mirrors the metaphysics of the world, matching up part for part. Ordinary or everyday talk (not to mention philosophical language) gets us into trouble according to this view, because the same word can be the sign for more than one thing, and different words can be the sign for the same thing. Worse, the underlying grammar of propositions is normally hidden from view. What is needed, Wittgenstein argues, is a logical language, a symbolism which obeys the rules of a logical grammar, not just an English or German grammar. The precision would keep us out of philosophical trouble, which is largely the result of grammatical or logical confusion.

Philosophical Investigations departs from all of this, and a thousand flowers bloom. Words are not signs which picture the world; instead they are thought of as tools, and their meanings derive from how we use them. We use words as variously as the many tools one might find in a toolbox, Wittgenstein says. Words can be used as differently as one might use a hammer, a screwdriver or a pot of glue. If words can be used in so many different ways, perhaps countless ways, meaning just has to break loose from the constraints urged in the *Tractatus*. It is a mistake, Wittgenstein argues, to think that words and logical relations must be sharply delineated, that meaning is built up of the component parts of a sentence, that truth depends on an exact modelling of reality. The old view falls apart, because in order to come to grips with language, one cannot try to pin it down to the world through logic, but must try to understand how words get used by living people.

Understanding a language, he claims in the *Investigations*, is not working out which objects particular words stand for, but knowing how to use words; it is an ability, not the result of analysis. There are different activities underway when we use words to give orders, describe objects, report events, speculate, hypothesize, act, sing, guess, joke, translate, ask, thank, curse or greet – Wittgenstein's list could conceivably go on for a while. We are doing different things when we engage in these activities, and our speech is a part of the activities themselves; the meaning of words is what it is because of the activities. Understanding a language, knowing what words mean, amounts to using words correctly against the backdrop of certain ways of carrying on as opposed to others. This is the largest insight in the *Investigations*. As Wittgenstein puts it, 'For a large class of cases – though not for all – in which we employ the word "meaning" it can be defined thus: the meaning of a word is its use in a language.'

Language-games

Wittgenstein claims that knowing how to use words is like knowing how to play a game, understanding the moves permitted and following the rules. He uses the term 'language-game' in many places 'to bring into prominence the fact that the *speaking* of language is part of an activity, or a form of life', as are the moves in a game. Wittgenstein talks about games themselves immediately after mentioning 'language-games', and the discussion is instructive. He asks us to examine all the activities we call 'games', and argues that they have no single essence, no one thing common to all in virtue of which they are all games. Consider card-games, board-games, ball-games, chess, noughts and crosses, tennis, a child simply throwing a ball against a wall and catching it – there is no essence here, no one thing in common. Instead, various games are related to one another in different ways; they share a kind of shifting similarity. Perhaps not everyone in the family album sports a version of grandmother's admirably high cheekbones, but there remains a kind of family resemblance made up of all sorts of different relations between the physical features of the members of a family. So too, Wittgenstein argues, with our concept of 'game'.

Using words in certain ways, language-games, are like this for Wittgenstein as well. There is no essence running through our use of words which makes them meaningful. The meaning comes from using words according to the rules of a certain practice. Using words is much like making moves in a game of chess. It does not make much sense to ask what the move (or the word) stands for or represents. To understand the 'meaning of the move', you need to know about the game, you need to have a grip on the point or purpose of the move. To know the meaning of a word, you need to know about the language-game in which it occurs, you need to have a grip on the point or purpose of its use. There is nothing more to know about the word.

You can get close to what Wittgenstein is up to in the *Investigations* by considering the following lines: 'How should we explain to someone what a game is? I imagine that we should describe *games* to him, and we might add: "This *and similar things* are called 'games".' And do we know any more about it ourselves?' It might be that the *Investigations* comes across as a series of sketches or remarks because Wittgenstein's attempt to explain the nature of language or deal with philosophical questions can only be descriptions of how we actually use words. On his view, what more could we do? What else could there be?

Dissolving philosophical problems

This conception of language gives Wittgenstein a method for dealing with philosophical problems. Such problems are not to be attempted or solved with theorizing, but dissolved by describing or examining our uses of words. Philosophical problems arise from linguistic confusions, mistaking the grammar of one kind of use for another or thinking that we bump into reality when we encounter nothing more than rules for the use of words – in general, trying to use a word incongruously, failing to play by the rules of a language-game. An example will make this clearer and, at the same time, go some way towards explaining how a theory of language can have implications for the rest of philosophy.

Wittgenstein's private language argument is not an argument in the usual sense – a series of premises and a conclusion – but a long discussion of what it might mean for someone to speak a private language. He starts by trying to imagine a language in which a person invents words which refer to what can only be known to the person herself, immediate or private sensations. Suppose every time she has a particular sensation, she writes 'S' in a notebook. Is 'S' now a word in her private language?

For a mark or a sound to have a meaning, on Wittgenstein's view, it has to have a use, and for it to have a use, there has to be a sense in which it might be misused. Marks and sounds get to have meaning against the backdrop of a system of use, a language-game, rules for going on in one way and not another, a form or way of life. But the person putting an 'S' in a notebook when she has a certain sensation is not participating in anything like this. Wittgenstein notes that in such a case the person has 'no criterion for correctness. One would like to say: whatever is going to seem right to me is right. And that only means that here we can't talk about "right"'. There is no external check, no way of determining that the mark is being used in any particular way and, without that, the mark is nothing more than a mark. The very idea of a private language is incoherent. The 'words' of a private language could not mean anything to us or to the person trying to speak it.

Rather dramatically, this line of thinking leads to the view that scepticism about the external world is entirely wrong-headed. Someone who argues that there is some doubt about the existence of external objects or other people is necessarily talking nonsense. For words to mean anything, they must have a use; and for words to have a use, there has to be a social context – there has to be a world with people in it, using language in a certain way. If you are persuaded by Wittgenstein's thinking here, you can start to wonder what Descartes was up to in the *Meditations*. You can also start worrying about what empiricists are talking about when they mention impressions and ideas or other sorts of private sensations known only to the mind containing them. On Wittgenstein's view, you will not discover much about inner objects or processes – thoughts, memories, sensations and the like – by introspecting or otherwise attending to them and reporting back. What needs attention is the use of the relevant words in our language.

Does this mean that our talk of thinking, pains, sensations, memories, and so on is necessarily nonsense too? Not at all. Wittgenstein is denying a certain conception of inner processes, a certain way of thinking of them, and he does so by attending to the use of our talk of such processes. Consider his treatment of remembering. Someone might claim that an inner process takes place when we remember, and that somehow we 'see it' happening. When I say that 'I remember something', the expression looks very much like what I say when I say that 'I see something' – but this superficial similarity does not make it true that there is the same kind of something out there and in here. What Wittgenstein wants to deny is not that there is an inner process happening, or even that there is a something inside our heads. What he wants to deny is that it is the inner process that we talk about when we talk about 'remembering'. This way of thinking about remembering stands in the way of our coming to understand how 'remembering' is used. And it is the use that matters. Once you have acquired the technique of using the word 'remember' in various language-games, you know everything there is to know about its meaning. There is nothing left to wonder about, but you might be deceived into thinking that there is if you still worry about the nature of an inner mental process. The worry is misplaced.

Philosophical worries in general are misplaced, on Wittgenstein's view, and perhaps it is this claim that matters most to him – certainly it is common to both the *Investigations* and the *Tractatus*. In the *Tractatus*, Wittgenstein argues that philosophy is not theorizing, not an attempt to describe the world, but is something akin to clarification. What gets clarified is not the truth about the world, but the view that nothing can be said about the world from a position external to it. What philosophy is usually thought to be about – answers to questions of value or questions about the nature of everything – is something impossible, or at least something we cannot express in a language. Philosophical questions demand answers which require a point of view outside the world, and logic and language cannot take us beyond the world. Understanding this amounts to realizing that the questions of philosophy are unanswerable – literally badly formed. Realizing this is realizing that there are no problems for philosophy to solve. You might be thinking that, therefore, the *Tractatus*, itself a work of philosophy, must be full of nonsense if Wittgenstein is right. He says as much:

My propositions serve as elucidations in the following way: anyone who understands me eventually recognizes them as nonsensical, when he has used them – as steps – to climb up beyond them. (He must, so to speak, throw away the ladder after he has climbed up it.)

The *Investigations* keeps the view that philosophical questions arise out of linguistic confusions, maintains that they are dissolved, not solved, by seeing language aright. But instead of pointing us to a correct conception of language and logic, Wittgenstein now immerses himself in language as it is, delights in the many uses of words in various language-games. Someone troubled by a philosophical worry – someone banging her head on the problems arising from, say, thinking that memories are private inner somethings – is not in need of a counter-argument. What she needs is to be reminded of how we use talk of memory, by considering the role our words have in language-games. Philosophy, for Wittgenstein, is language on holiday, and it is the job of those who have seen the light to get language back to work by reminding us of how we actually use it.

Bibliography

Primary Sources

Versions of the works considered in this book are available in most good bookshops. There are book series, for example Penguin Classics, which contain inexpensive and generally reasonable versions of the relevant texts, sometimes with useful introductory material. There are also larger, scholarly collections of the complete works of a given philosopher, usually found in university and other libraries but sometimes available in bookshops as well. The following is a list of primary sources, indicating readily available and usually standard versions of the great books and, where appropriate, reliable translations. When coming to a philosopher for the first time, though, there is nothing wrong with simply opting for the cheaper version in a book series.

Aquinas (1993), T. McDermott (ed.), *Aquinas: Selected Writings*. Oxford: Oxford University Press.

Aristotle (1984), 'Nicomachean Ethics', in J. Barnes (ed.), *The Complete Works of Aristotle: The Revised Oxford Translation*. 2 vols. Princeton: Princeton University Press.

Ayer, A. J. (1946), *Language, Truth and Logic*. 2nd edition. London: Gollancz.

Berkeley, G. (1975), 'Principles of Human Knowledge', in M. Ayers (ed.), *Philosophical Works*. London: Dent.

de Beauvoir, Simone (1989), H. M. Parshley (trans), *The Second Sex*. New York: Vintage.

Descartes, R. (1996), J. Cottingham (trans, ed.), *Meditations on First Philosophy*. Cambridge: Cambridge University Press.

Hegel, G. W. F. (1977), A. V. Miller (trans), *The Phenomenology of Spirit*. Oxford: Oxford University Press.

Hobbes, T. (1996), K. Schumann and G. A. J. Rogers (eds), *Leviathan*. Oxford: Oxford University Press.

Hume, D. (1975), 'An Enquiry Concerning Human Understanding' in L. A. Selby-Bigge (ed.), 3rd edition revised by P. H. Nidditch, *Enquiries Concerning Human Understanding and Concerning the Principles of Morals*. Oxford: Clarendon Press.

Kant, I. (1929), N. Kemp Smith (trans), *Critique of Pure Reason*. New York: St Martin's Press.

Locke, J. (1975), P. H. Nidditch (ed.), *An Essay Concerning Human Understanding*. Oxford: Clarendon Press.

Marx, K. (2000), 'The Communist Manifesto' in D. McLennan (ed.), *Karl Marx: Selected Writings*. Oxford: Oxford University Press.

Mill, J. S. (1963), 'Utilitarianism', in J. M. Robson (ed.), *Collected Works of John Stuart Mill*. Toronto: University of Toronto Press.

Nietzsche, F. (1968), 'Thus Spoke Zarathustra', in W. Kaufmann (trans), *The Portable Nietzsche*. New York: Viking Press.

Plato (1989), *Republic*, in E. Hamilton and H. Cairns (eds), *Plato: The Collected Dialogues*. Princeton: Princeton University Press.

Popper, K. (1959), *The Logic of Scientific Discovery*. London: Hutchinson.

Rousseau, J. (1997), 'The Social Contract' in Victor Gourevitch (ed.), *Rousseau: 'The Social Contract' and Other Later Political Writings*. Cambridge: Cambridge University Press.

Sartre, J. P. (1948), H. E. Barnes (trans), *Being and Nothingness*. New York: Philosophical Library.

Schopenhauer, A. (1966), E. J. F. Payne (trans), *The World as Will and Representation*. New York: Dover.

Wittgenstein, L. (1953), G. E. M. Anscombe (trans) and R. Rhees (eds), *Philosophical Investigations*. Oxford: Blackwell.

Secondary Sources

The secondary literature is vast. The following will help you into it, and many of the works listed inform the chapters of this book. I have restricted myself to around five secondary sources for each of the great books, along with some good general reference books. I have omitted journal articles which, though helpful, might not be easy to obtain outside of university libraries. I have also chosen only books which are still in print or books you at least stand a reasonable chance of finding in a library. I have thought, too, about the usefulness of the books for the beginning student. Even so, some of the books listed are difficult.

Ackrill, J. L. (1991), *Aristotle the Philosopher*. Oxford: Oxford University Press.

Allison, H. (1983), *Kant's Transcendental Idealism*. New Haven: Yale University Press.

Anderson, T. (1993), *Sartre's Two Ethics: From Authenticity to Integral Humanity*. Chicago: Open Court.

Anscombe, G. E. M. (1959), *An Introduction to Wittgenstein's Tractatus*. London: Hutchinson.

Arrington, R. (1999) (ed.), *A Companion to the Philosophers*. Malden, MA: Blackwell.

Atwell, J. (1995), *Schopenhauer on the Character of the World*. Berkeley: University of California Press.

Austin, J. L. (1962), *Sense and Sensibilia*. Oxford: Clarendon Press.

Ayers, M. (1991), *Locke: Epistemology and Ontology*. London: Routledge.

Barnes, J. (1995) (ed.), *The Cambridge Companion to Aristotle*. Cambridge: Cambridge University Press.

—— (2000), *A Very Short Introduction to Aristotle*. Oxford: Oxford University Press.

Beauchamp, T. L. and A. Rosenberg (1981), *Hume and the Problem of Causation*. Oxford: Oxford University Press.

Bennett, J. (1971), *Locke, Berkeley, Hume: Central Themes*. Oxford: Oxford University Press.

Berghoffen, D. (1996), *The Philosophy of Simone de Beauvoir: Gendered Phenomenologies, Erotic Generosities*. New York: SUNY Press.

Blackburn, S. (1994) (ed.), *The Oxford Dictionary of Philosophy*. Oxford: Oxford University Press.

Catalano, J. (1980), *A Commentary of Jean-Paul Sartre's Being and Nothingness*. Chicago: University of Chicago Press.

Chappell, V. (1994), *The Cambridge Companion to Locke*. Cambridge: Cambridge University Press.

—— (1997), *Descartes' Meditations: Critical Essays*. Lanham: Rowan & Littlefield.

Cohen, G. A. (2001), *Karl Marx's Theory of History: A Defence*. Oxford: Oxford University Press.

Coppleston, F. C. (1955), *Aquinas*. London: Penguin Books.

—— (1946–75), *A History of Philosophy*. 9 vols. London: Search Press.

Cottingham, J. (1992), *The Cambridge Companion to Descartes*. Cambridge: Cambridge University Press.

—— (1998) (ed.), *Descartes*. Oxford: Oxford University Press.

Cranston, M. (1991), *The Nobel Savage: Jean-Jacques Rousseau*. Chicago: University of Chicago Press.

Dancy, J. (1987), *Berkeley: an Introduction*. Oxford: Blackwell.

Donner, W. (1991), *The Liberal Self: John Stuart Mill's Moral and Political Philosophy*. Ithaca: Cornell University Press.

Elders, L. (1990), *The Philosophical Theology of St. Thomas Aquinas*. New York: E. J. Brill.

Elster, J. (1985), *Making Sense of Marx*. Cambridge: Cambridge University Press.

Feyerabend, P. (1975), *Against Method*. London: New Left Books.

Fine, G. (1999), *Plato 2: Ethics, Politics, Religion, and the Soul*. Oxford: Oxford University Press.

Fogelin, R. J. (1985), *Hume's Scepticism in the Treatise of Human Nature*. London: Routledge.

—— (2001), *Berkeley and the Principles of Human Knowledge*. London: Routledge.

Forster, M. N. (1998), *Hegel's Idea of a Phenomenology of Spirit*. Chicago: University of Chicago Press.

Foster, J. (1985), *A. J. Ayer*. London: Routledge.

Gardner, S. (1998), *Routledge Philosophy Guidebook to Kant and the Critique of Pure Reason*. London: Routledge.

Gauthier, D. P. (1969), *The Logic of Leviathan: the Moral and Political Theory of Thomas Hobbes*. Oxford: Oxford University Press.

Grayling, A. C. (1996), *Berkeley: The Central Arguments*. Oxford: Oxford University Press.

Glock, J. (1996), *A Wittgenstein Dictionary*. Oxford: Blackwell.

Griffiths, A. P. (ed.) (1991), *A. J. Ayer Memorial Essays*. Cambridge: Cambridge University Press.

Guyer, P. (1992) (ed.), *The Cambridge Companion to Kant*. Cambridge: Cambridge University Press.

Hacker, P. M. S. (1996), *Wittgenstein's Place in Twentieth Century Analytic Philosophy*. Oxford: Blackwell.

Hamlyn, D. (1980), *Schopenhauer*. London: Routledge.

Hampton, J. (1986), *Hobbes and the Social Contract Tradition*. Cambridge: Cambridge University Press.

Hanfling, O. (1999), *Ayer*. London: Routledge.

Hankey, W. J. (1987), *God in Himself: Aquinas' Doctrine of God as Expounded in the Summa Theologiae*. Oxford: Oxford University Press.

Higgins, K. M. (1987), *Nietzsche's Zarathustra*. Philadelphia: Temple University Press.

Honderich, T. (1991) (ed.), *Essays on A. J. Ayer*. Cambridge: Cambridge University Press.

—— (1995) (ed.), *The Oxford Companion to Philosophy*. Oxford: Oxford University Press.

Houlgate, S. (1991), *Freedom, Truth and History: An Introduction to Hegel's Philosophy*. London: Routledge.

Inwood, M. (1983), *Hegel*. London: Routledge.

Irwin, T. (1995), *Plato's Ethics*. Oxford: Oxford University Press.

Jacquette, D. (1996) (ed.), *Schopenhauer, Philosophy and the Arts*. Cambridge: Cambridge University Press.

Janaway, C. (1994), *Schopenhauer*. Oxford: Oxford University Press.

Jeanson, F. (1981), R. Stone (trans), *Sartre and the Problem of Morality*. Bloomington: Indiana University Press.

Kavka, G. S. (1986), *Hobbesian Moral and Political Theory*. Princeton: Princeton University Press.

Kenny, A. (1968), *Descartes: A Study of His Philosophy*. Bristol: Thommes Press.

—— (1973), *Wittgenstein*. Cambridge: Harvard University Press.

Kuhn, T. S. (1962), *The Structure of Scientific Revolutions*. Chicago: University of Chicago Press.

Lakatos, I. (1978), J. Worral and G. Currie (eds), *The Methodology of*

Scientific Research Programmes. Cambridge: Cambridge University Press.

Lambert, L. (1987), *Nietzsche's Teaching: an Interpretation of Thus Spoke Zarathustra*. New Haven: Yale University Press.

Lowe, E. J. (1995), *Locke on Human Understanding*. London: Routledge.

Mackie, J. L. (1976), *Problems from Locke*. Oxford: Clarendon Press.

Magnus, B. and K. M. Higgins. (1996) (eds), *The Cambridge Companion to Nietzsche*. Cambridge: Cambridge University Press.

McBride, W. L. (1997) (ed.), *Sartre and Existentialism*. 8 vols. New York: Garland.

McCabe, M. M. (1994), *Plato's Individuals*. Princeton: Princeton University Press.

McGinn, C. (1984), *Wittgenstein on Meaning*. Oxford: Blackwell.

McInerny, R. (2004), *Aquinas*. Cambridge: Polity Press.

Miller, D. (1994), *Critical Rationalism: A Restatement and Defence*. Chicago: Open Court.

Muehlmann, R. G. (1992), *Berkeley's Ontology*. Indianapolis: Hackett.

Norton, D. F. (1993) (ed.), *The Cambridge Companion to Hume*. Cambridge: Cambridge University Press.

Nussbaum, M. C. (1980), *The Fragility of Goodness*. Cambridge: Cambridge University Press.

O'Hagan, T. (1999), *Rousseau*. London: Routledge.

O'Hear, A. (1980), *Karl Popper*. London: Routledge.

Pears, D. (1990), *Hume's System: an Examination of the First Book of His Treatise*. Oxford: Oxford University Press.

Riley, P. (2001) (ed.), *The Cambridge Companion to Rousseau*. Cambridge: Cambridge University Press.

Rorty, A. O. (1980), *Essays on Aristotle's Ethics*. Berkeley: University of California Press.

Roth, J. K. (2000) (ed.), *World Philosophers and Their Works*. Pasadena, CA and Hackensack, NJ: Salem Press.

Russell, B. (1961), *A History of Western Philosophy*. London: Allen & Unwin.

Santoni, R. E. (1995), *Bad Faith, Good Faith and Authenticity in Sartre's Early Philosophy*. Philadelphia: Temple University Press.

Schlipp, P. A. (1981) (ed.), *The Philosophy of Jean-Paul Sartre*. La Salle: Open Court.

Schneewind, J. B. (1997), *The Invention of Autonomy: History of Modern Moral Philosophy*. Cambridge: Cambridge University Press.

Scruton, R. (1982), *Kant*. Oxford: Oxford University Press.

—— (1996), *Modern Philosophy*. London: Mandarin Paperbacks.

Simons, M. (1995) (ed.), *Feminist Interpretations of Simone de Beauvoir*. University Park: Pennsylvania State University Press.

Singer, P. (2000), *Marx: A Very Short Introduction*. Oxford: Oxford University Press.

Skorupski, J. (1989), *John Stuart Mill*. London: Routledge.

—— (1998) (ed.), *The Cambridge Companion to John Stuart Mill*. Cambridge: Cambridge University Press.

Sluga, H. and D Stern. (1996) (eds), *The Cambridge Companion to Wittgenstein*. Cambridge: Cambridge University Press.

Sorrell, T. (1987), *Descartes*. Oxford: Oxford University Press.

—— (1996) (ed.), *The Cambridge Companion to Hobbes*. Cambridge: Cambridge University Press.

Stern, R. (2002), *Routledge Philosophy Guidebook to Hegel and the Phenomenology of Spirit*. London: Routledge.

Strawson, G. (1989), *The Secret Connection: Causation, Realism and David Hume*. Oxford: Oxford University Press.

Strawson, P. F. (1966), *The Bounds of Sense: An Essay on Kant's Critique of Pure Reason*. London: Methuen.

Stroud, B. (1977), *Hume*. London: Routledge.

Stump, E. (2003), *Aquinas*. London: Routledge.

Tanner, M. (1994), *Nietzsche*. Oxford: Oxford University Press.

Tuck, R. (1989), *Hobbes*. Oxford: Oxford University Press.

Vlastos, G. (1994), *Studies in Greek Philosophy*. Princeton: Princeton University Press.

Walsh, W. H. (1975), *Kant's Criticism of Metaphysics*. Edinburgh: Edinburgh University Press.

Williams, B. (1978), *Descartes: The Project of Pure Enquiry*. London: Penguin Books.

Wilson, F. (1990), *Psychological Analysis and the Philosophy of John Stuart Mill*. Toronto: University of Toronto Press.

Winkler, K. P. (1989), *Berkeley: An Interpretation*. Oxford: Clarendon Press.

Wolff, J. (2002), *Why Read Marx Today?* Oxford: Oxford University Press.

Wolker, R. (1995) (ed.), *Rousseau and Liberty*. Manchester: Manchester University Press.

Wood, A. (1981), *Karl Marx*. London: Routledge.

Woolhouse, R. S. (1983), *Locke*. Minneapolis: University of Minnesota Press.

Index